THE YEAR OF DRINKING MAGIC

TWELVE CEREMONIES WITH THE VINE OF SOULS

GUY CRITTENDEN

APOCRYPHILE
PRESS

Apocryphile Press
1700 Shattuck Ave #81
Berkeley, CA 94709
www.apocryphile.org

© Copyright 2017 by Guy Crittenden
Printed in the United States of America
ISBN 978-1-944769-98-7

The author will donate all his royalties from the sale of this book to the Amazon Rainforest Conservancy (ARC) www.amazonrainforest-conservancy.com

Cover and author photo by Vlad Kamenski of Evans Photography in Toronto, Canada. www.evansphotography.ca

Snake illustration based on Guy Crittenden's tattoo, inked by Daemon Rowanchilde in Maple Leaf, Ontario. www.urbanprimitive.com

These stories portray real people and events, but the names and some circumstantial details have been changed to protect privacy.

Please join our mailing list at
www.apocryphilepress.com/free
and we'll keep you up-to-date on all our new releases
—and we'll also send you a FREE BOOK. Visit us today!

Contents

For my sons Wilson and Jackson.
For when you need these blazes
on your individual trails.

Last night, as I was sleeping,
I dreamt — marvelous error! —
that I had a beehive
here inside my heart.
And the golden bees
were making white combs
and sweet honey
from my old failures.

—ANTONIO MACHADO

I can't embark on this account without thanking at least a few people without whose insights and kindness the interpretation of these strange events would be impossible.

First there are my teachers — some living, some dead — whose explanations of shamanism, spirituality, ancient texts and psychedelic experience have been invaluable.

Among these the late lecturer on comparative religions Alan Watts ranks highly; his explanations of Eastern philosophy laid the groundwork for my understanding of what has befallen me. His talks and writings about the Hindu concept that we are all "God in disguise" was essential for me after the psychedelic plants pulled down the egoic structures of my mind.

The lectures and books of Ram Dass (Richard Alpert) have similarly informed, and also taught me the importance of *taking life's curriculum*, tying me to the mast against the psychedelic sirens as ends in themselves, or the temptation to drop out of society completely after I learned, well... what I learned.

I'm perhaps most indebted to the late Terence McKenna, who died in 1999 at age 55 (my age when I began this book). McKenna, an American psychonaut, culture commentator and "scientist without portfolio" convinced me through books like *True Hallucinations* and his (literally) hundreds of recorded talks to embrace the psychedelic path with a fearlessness I likely otherwise would not have summoned.

I commend to everyone a few other souls whose works have helped immensely. In no particular order there's Cambridge biologist Rupert Sheldrake, whose concept of "morphogenic fields" mightily informs my own ideas about consciousness (which may not be restricted to the inside of our skulls). There's the punk rock bass player and ordained Soto Zen monk Brad Warner, whose books — though "anti-psychedelic" — gave me my deepest insights into Buddhism. I can't say enough good things about his explanations of the writings of the 13th Century monk Dogen (the Sir Isaac Newton of Buddhism) and his elaborations that we're all local manifestations of a universal, non-local consciousness. This idea is supported by the writings and talks of physicist Amit Goswami, whose book and documentary *The Quantum Physicist* has also influenced me. Extending that is Ervin Laszlo's masterpiece *Science and the Akashic Field: An Integral Theory of Everything* — which substantiated my intuition that physics and spirituality are now supporting one another, if not quite merging. Former NASA physicist Tom Campbell's book *My Big TOE* (Theory of Everything) is thought provoking and we independently arrived at the same video game metaphor to describe the very real possibility that we're all living inside a simulation. Stem cell biologist Bruce Lipton's bestselling book *The Biology of Belief* is also congruent with some of my intuitions, especially his insights about the way receptors on the membrane of cells glean information from the environment and may be the "brain" of cells as much as anything inside.

Perhaps no single book convinced me to actually ingest shamanic visionary plants more than Graham Hancock's excellent *Supernatural:*

Meetings with the Ancient Teachers of Mankind. Hancock combines lively accounts of his own experiments with a variety of plants with in-depth research of ancient artifacts and cave paintings, making a convincing case for shamans in our deep past having used psychotropic plants to access altered states of consciousness, ultimately triggering the development of civilization (which may be older than currently thought).

Local friends who've been supportive of my journey know who they are and I won't attempt to list them all. But I must send a shout-out to Dan Cleland — former owner of Pulse Tours — whose company was doula to my shamanic rebirth in the jungles of Peru, and which generously sponsored this book's initial crowdfunding campaign on Publishizer. And thanks to all the other travellers on that life-changing trip, with whom I've remained friends: Tatyana, Sid, Mike, Jun Jun (my roommate there), Carl and Mike (whose book about the trip, *Ayahuasca: An Executive's Enlightenment*, I helped bring out under my Sage & Feather Press imprint, and the content of which allows me to recount that adventure in less granular detail here).

Thanks also to my yoga teacher friend Caroline Coyle for introducing me to Sufi whirling dance, and to musician and spiritual teacher Darren Austin Hall, and Tricia Sabo, both of whom led me to American shaman Bradford Keeney — the great teacher of the shaking medicine of the Kalahari bushmen, whose First Creation cosmology holds eerie parallels with the realms accessed via Amazon plant shamanism. Thanks also to "death doula" and friend Carole Trepanier for suggesting *huachuma* (San Pedro cactus) — the "ayahuasca of the day" that was sacred to the Inca — and for her guidance in interpreting journeys that increasingly became self-induced NDEs (near death experiences).

Other friends who deserve special mention include plant expert Timothy Martin, visionary art scholar Angela O'Hara, Celtic harpist and shaman Brendan Ring, musical and healing duo Bolormaa and Tiger, spiritual guides Natasha and Sherri Lupus, my healer friend Bobbi McWilliams and my special DMT neo-shaman friend who, in this book, is named Nefertiti.

To those whom I've thoughtlessly omitted from this list, I offer an apology and much gratitude.

And finally here I must offer a warning and a disclaimer. This book records *my* experiences working with the sacred plant medicine. Although certain archetypal themes reappear time and again among people who drink ayahuasca, each person's experience is fundamentally unique. If you choose to drink the vine of souls, your journey may seem purely physical and include no visions at all. (And be cautioned that visions are not the be-all and end-all of this experience). You may or may not receive extraordinary healing, and you could, in fact, feel *nothing at all*. (I've seen it happen.) You may choose the medicine, but it might not choose *you* (at least, not at first).

Many factors contribute to or impinge upon the ayahuasca experience, as with other psychotropic plants. Your mood and psychology at the time are a factor, as well as the *set and setting*. Some might say that where your soul is in its journey, in this incarnation, is also a factor. And ayahuasca nights can vary wildly from one to another, even for just one person.

I caution readers to thoroughly research and vet curanderos or other facilitators with whom they may choose to sit. Word of mouth is invaluable. (And I profoundly advise against anyone drinking ayahuasca alone — at least until they've become very experienced.) You have choices in front of you, including whether to seek the medicine in your home country or travel to South America for the fuller experience. And even then, it's a bit of a Wild West in places like Peru, where the quality and safety of what's on offer varies widely. Price is not a reliable indicator of much other than perhaps the comfort level of the accommodations.

If a person seeks healing for a profound illness, I'd caution that the *tourist style* kind of trip I went on might not be suitable. Whether their healing takes place in a luxury retreat center or in some hovel is less important than the skill and experience of the curandero. Remember that traditionally ayahuasca was primarily a *diagnostic tool* used by Amazonian shamans in much the way doctors use x-rays in the industrialized world. The curandero would drink the medicine in order to see what's wrong, then head into the forest with a machete to find the right plant or bark for a salve or curative potion. A genuine curandero will look after you as a whole person, spiritually and physically.

So, if you seek treatment for a serious illness, be prepared for a longer stay and to potentially consume other medicines. In the documentary film *The Sacred Science*, eight people spend a month in the jungle and attain a range of outcomes, some of them very positive. That feels about right to me. That being said, drinking ayahuasca yourself could help you understand your medical condition better, as long as you're screened for being well enough to try it. In my experience, some people with issues like PTSD, depression, anxiety or addiction can achieve positive results in an accelerated time frame.

Again, your mileage may vary.

I also don't claim that ayahuasca or any visionary plant is the only way to attain the kind of healing and spiritual awakening described in this book. I have no doubt that traditional shamanic drumming, African shaking medicine, seated meditation, yoga, Sufi whirling and other modalities can lead to extraordinary insights and enlightenment. It's just that Amazonian plant shamanism called *me*, and is an important part of *my* path. As you'll see in the Epilogue, I'm also interested in the other modalities, both to support my work with the plants and also as worthwhile pathways in themselves.

One last thing needs to be said before we turn to my story. An occurrence at a family gathering offered a sobering lesson.

I was sitting at a restaurant table with extended family who'd traveled from far and wide a couple of years ago to celebrate my mother's 80th birthday. I remarked on some concept as being too New-Agey for my thinking, which launched a twitter of laughter at the table.

In that moment I realized I was a figure of ridicule, the point being that anything too "out there" even for me must truly be crazy. This spoke volumes about the attitude of these relatives — who are thoughtful and kind people — toward my critical thinking skills and gullibility. Clearly they believed my reports of working with shamanic plants and visionary experience were evidence of my having become a somewhat woo-woo Shirley MacLaine-style New Age spiritualist.

This is one part of what I call the *shaman's burden*. When we enter into the kinds of experiences described in this book, we're dealing not only with subjects with which most people are unfamiliar, but that fall into the category of real superstition, properly understood as those things about which people are *unaware even that they're unaware*. Many intrepid psychonauts have mentioned this in the past, and it's the reason many shamans are secretive about what they encounter.

It's worth stating here, then, that (for the record) I'm actually a deeply skeptical person. I'm science- and evidence-oriented, and am not at all the kind of person drawn intuitively to the world of crystals, oracle cards, magic wands and unicorns. I came to my interest in spirituality via the unlikely route of readings in quantum physics, and such strange phenomena as quantum entanglement, quantum tunneling, and the results of the famous double-slit experiment (and the more recent delayed-choice quantum eraser).

In truth, I bristle when people ask me my *sign* and fish around for astrological explanations of me or anything else (though I recognize that Carl Jung respected that science or art form for its archetypal potency; it is, after all, an internally consistent self-referential system like chess or mathematics). I'm not one who easily feels shifts in "the energy" (whatever *that* is) or imagines that some anointed few who've read *The Celestine Prophecy* are about to ascend to a crystalline fifth dimension. For most of my life I was quite a hardcore atheist and took pride (and still do) in being an existentialist in the Albert Camus mold.

But I am a *possibilist* and rule out nothing until disproven. It was only when I *experientially* endured and enjoyed the opening up of different dimensions of consciousness via shamanic plants that I began reporting on the paranormal-seeming events that even I concede can sound mightily like the spiritual babble my relatives chuckled over at the dinner table.

And so I declare at the outset that I make no claims whatsoever about the ultimate reality and provenance of the experiences herein described. I simply do my best to faithfully record and share what I saw, felt and thought, moment by moment, as I went through each ayahuasca ceremony, like an honest journalist reporting any other eye-witness account. I do speculate from time to time about what the experiences mean, and whether they're of an objective reality or merely drug-induced hallucinations all *inside my head*. But my opinions are lightly held; they're simply my working theory at the present time.

And with that caveat, we turn to our story...

So many people live within unhappy circumstances and yet will not take the initiative to change their situation because they are conditioned to a life of security, conformity, and conservatism, all of which may appear to give one peace of mind, but in reality nothing is more dangerous to the adventurous spirit within a man than a secure future. The very basic core of a man's living spirit is his passion for adventure. The joy of life comes from our encounters with new experiences, and hence there is no greater joy than to have an endlessly changing horizon, for each day to have a new and different sun.

— JON KRAKAUER, *Into the Wild*

...All the psychedelic stuff faded and in a large square area in the center of my visual plane I saw a vignette that looked like a shaky old Super 8 home movie.

It was my mother, Yvonne, playing golf. She was wearing a golf visor and her eyes beamed. She was clearly enjoying herself, and I was able to look closely at her eyes. They were directing love and attention toward some person "off camera."

11

It was startlingly realistic.

Sometimes it's difficult to conjure up a detailed recollection of a person's face. We think we can do it, but if you stop and try, randomly, it's actually difficult to reconstruct a person's features in great detail, even those of close relatives. (Sometimes people get upset after a loved-one dies, castigating themselves that they can't remember what they looked like.) But in this instance I saw my mother as if she were right in front of me. It was a sunny day and she was happy.

After this vision disappeared I lay back and contemplated what it meant.

It was very strange. To start with, my mother doesn't play golf. In the vision she appeared younger than her age at the time of the vision — perhaps in her late forties, I'd guess.

Then I figured it out, and the realization hit me hard.

The universal consciousness was showing me my mother enjoying another life — a different life than the one she chose.

In this other life, she'd married someone other than my father. I was seeing her enjoying herself with other people in a world into which I'd never been born, a world in which she was not my mother.

There are few things more painful than seeing your own mother enjoying a life in which she never became your mom.

All at once I felt the poignancy of our bond as it (thankfully) exists, and the "near miss" of my never having been born.

Why I was being shown this was self-evident: It was all about appreciation, and I felt gratitude. Immense gratitude.

We focus so much on the various ways our parents fail or disappoint us, without appreciating enough our good fortune in ever having landed a place in the realm of the embodied in the first place.

I was then taken on a whirlwind tour of her marriages to her first and second husbands. I got to see how the universe conspired to create me. Even the toughest experiences I endured growing up — the emotional abandonment or abuse I felt at times — was all part of a program to prepare me for my destiny.

It's impossible to fully convey the nuance of this lesson. In the end, the lesson was for me, and for me only. It wasn't some kind of intellectualization either, but more of a felt experience. I found myself longing... longing for what actually happened...

This description, from my eleventh ayahuasca ceremony, speaks to the soul of this book, which reports my own direct experiences without too much speculation on their implications about the fundamental nature of reality, though I do contemplate that in places. Ayahuasca is a dualistic teacher plant, offering lessons in light and dark, heaven and hell, male and female... always yin and yang (or more accurately, inseparable yin-yang). She has always appeared to me as a female spirit, and many of her lessons have concerned the feminine: women, lovers, my mother, mothers in general, the universal mother and, ultimately, Gaia herself.

* * *

This book is a message in a bottle to the next generation, placed gently by the midwife of dreams in the lamplit tide of a dying world. I yearn for a regenerated planet and a human civilization reinvented with new forms of consciousness...

...yet my heart tamps with doubt.

Earth herself won't disappear — the spinning rock that incubated us will endure for billions more years before she's swallowed by the sun. By then we'll have left on starships or will have evolved into something else. Maybe we'll traverse space inter-dimensionally.

That is, if we make it through the current ecological crisis. We're living in the Anthropocene: the Earth's latest mass extinction event. The full impact of climate change has yet to be felt, yet as I write this, already 50 per cent of all life that existed on this planet when I was born in 1960 has vanished.

Desperate times call for desperate measures. The situation spurred me to seek out the ancient wisdom of mankind — even of the Earth herself — in shamanic ceremony with teacher plants.

I'd spent 25 years as an environmental journalist, editing magazines on pollution control and municipal and commercial recycling. I knew all about the technocratic solutions to the consumer society's impacts on natural systems. And it's true that industrial ecology can thereby stem many of the problems that threaten ecosystems and human wellbeing.

But none of it will be enough.

The destruction of nature is *baked into* our predatory style of capitalism and the neocon/neoliberal economics that has dismantled the welfare state in industrialized countries over the past 35 years. Each month it expropriates the funds needed for sustainable development and green energy to finance perpetual wars instead — illegal wars against sovereign states that are (unsurprisingly) always rich in oil, or against terrorist groups that usually have strange ties to Western intelligence agencies.

And so I felt called to drink *ayahuasca* — the *vine of souls* — and learn whether or not its lessons could help unlock the secrets I needed to understand both in terms of personal healing or spiritual insight, and in terms of solutions to our current global predicament.

But that isn't the whole truth.

If I'm to be honest, my own aging and fear of and wonderment about death was central in my decision to drink *ayahuasca* — the *vine of the dead.*

My stepfather had died the year before, and I was fed up with the shallow explanations of death in my own culture, which were really *explaining away...*

I wanted to know if ayahuasca might reveal, or at least offer clues, about what happens to us when we shuffle off this mortal coil.

Do we have souls? Are we immortal? Is reincarnation real? What is the afterlife *like*?

My experience with the vine was profound, vastly exceeding anything for which I could have hoped or been prepared.

Soon after my first-ever participation in an ayahuasca ceremony, I thought, "I'll spend the rest of my life trying to understand what happened in just the first ten minutes of this experience."

And this appears to be true.

I've consumed the shamanic brew many times since drinking it the first time on New Year's Eve at the end of 2013 in the main *maloka* (ceremonial building) at the Nihue Rao Spiritual Center outside Iquitos, Peru. Though the visions and themes of the tryptamine space are more familiar to me now, ayahuasca's revelations continue to challenge and overturn my assumptions about what consciousness is and about the nature of reality.

I now refer to the visionary plants as *necroptics* because, in the way they affect me, they trigger a near-death experience or NDE. Ayahuasca has become quite literally the vine of *my soul*. The vine of *my death*. And other shamanic plants now affect me this way, too.

Shortly before I departed on that fateful journey in 2013, my friend Aaron said, "There will be a Guy Crittenden who gets on the plane to Peru, and another Guy Crittenden who returns." That statement was more prescient than either of us realized at the time.

The medicine healed and transformed me to an amazing extent, offering teachings I hadn't thought possible from a plant. Most importantly it also opened up my "Third Eye" and I can now journey in the shamanic realms to varying degrees with or without medicine. The healing and transformation was so profound that I now refer to myself sometimes (jokingly) as *Guy Crittenden 2.0*.

Yes, that person is dead, at least partially. He feels more like a role I play in a costume drama. Sometimes it pains me to perform him overly much, especially when pressed to do so by old friends and relatives, who remain somewhat oblivious to my transformation. Can I blame them, really, for offering a piece of leaf to the old caterpillar, when the butterfly's wings are hidden?

I perform the old role as needed and try to offer a glad heart, but in secret, I dance, I whirl like a skeleton above a grave. They have no idea how many times I've died.

In Peru I drank ayahuasca three times. A couple of months after I returned, I started experiencing a series of uncanny phenomena that further investigation revealed were *shamanic* in nature. These ranged from the appearance late at night of colors and complex geometric patterns, to shimmering white light reminiscent of the Aurora Borealis moving over my whole body, to the sudden appearance in my field of vision of fully-realized detailed landscapes.

The phenomena also included auditory hallucinations, such as my being awoken in the wee hours by the sound of a wildcat tearing apart its prey in the bedroom hallway, and phrases offered to me from some apparent spirit realm in a language I don't speak, which subsequent investigation revealed had specific and profound meaning.

I have also experienced the so-called "11:11 phenomenon" in a particularly intense way. Synchronicities show up in my life with uncanny frequency. At times the incidents have had a haunting quality, as though I'm shifting between quantum realities.

For strangeness, perhaps no phenomenon rivals the regular appearance, at any time of the night or day, of a spirit animal that begins as a tiny point of brilliant light in the distance, then gets bigger and bigger until it fills almost my whole visual field — making it difficult or impossible to drive or read text in a book or on a computer screen — before it enters the top of my head, the crown chakra.

These strange phenomena spurred me to investigate spiritual and paranormal literature and seek out people experienced in shamanism and disciplines like yoga, African shaking medicine and Sufi whirling.

Investigation revealed that what I initially feared was some kind of brain damage was instead symptomatic of spiritual breakthroughs, shamanic journeys.

Simply put, I was undergoing an *awakening*.

But to what?

Ayahuasca opened a kind of portal into otherly dimensions of consciousness — the same realms experienced by shamans when they enter trance states through drumming or ecstatic dance, and akin to what yogis call *kundalini*. Exotic developments took place inside me that are normally attained only via years of demanding physical and meditative practice.

Within a year of returning from Peru, I left my 25-year career editing environmental business magazines in order to devote myself full-time to my newfound mystical pursuits, as well as to activism in support of environmental and humanitarian issues.

Every area of my life has been touched and transformed. I'm now vegan. I've swapped out my conventional buttoned-up clothing for more relaxed yoga wear. I avoid the fluoride in tap water, rumored to calcify the pineal gland — presumed home of the Third Eye.

My body now bears a large tribal-style tattoo inspired by the Q'ero anaconda deity Pachamama, also known in her aspects of sky (Wayramama), earth (Sachamama) and water (Yukamama). She spirals down my left arm from shoulder to hand. She is the spirit animal that visits me. She is the goddess I serve.

* * *

I resisted writing this book.

It seems like everyone is writing a book about ayahuasca these days, and the medicine has been reported in mainstream media such as CNN and the *New York Times*. In truth, I was also afraid that the spirit of ayahuasca herself would be angry — about my hubris. (She has ways of punishing egotism, trust me!)

But as late as my 2013 trip, detailed accounts of ayahuasca journeys were still sparse. Most (even now) read like typical "trip reports" of people's LSD experiences in the 1970s, with very few offering any kind of *shamanic* interpretation. Indeed, even though many storytellers have drunk the medicine in the presence of a *curandero* (the Peruvian term for "healer" or shaman), many appear to know little about shamanism.

This is ironic, since ayahuasca is a powerful gateway to shamanic experience.

I feel called to share my experiences with others, via this book, as the paranormal or psychedelic experiences continue to thrust themselves upon me. In fact, the medicine itself has compelled me to do so.

People in the technocratic societies of North America, Europe and elsewhere need to know about the other dimension (or dimensions) of reality that runs parallel to the one we normally inhabit.

Whether those dimensions are "out there" somewhere or whether it's "all in one's head" is a longstanding issue hotly debated in the psychedelic community. My own view is that it doesn't really matter, and I suspect anyway that both are true, that there is no "outer" world and "inner" world; intuition tells me they're spectrums of *one reality*.

I think of our experience of ordinary three-dimensional reality as being like a television set to channel seven. We live most of our lives experiencing only that channel, and assume that's all there is. Psychotropic plants allow mysterious signals from, say, channel six or channel eight to filter in, making us aware there's more information available than the programming with which we're familiar.

This was common knowledge among the indigenous people whose societies have been largely genocided by the imperial cultures of the colonial era over the past 500 years. Our technocratic societies continue to view the *superstitions* of indigenous cultures with disdain. Their beliefs must be based on ignorance, we assume, and their health treatments cannot, surely, compare with those of *modern medicine*. Any positive effects must only be from the placebo effect…

The Wachowski siblings' *Matrix* film trilogy provides an apt metaphor for our mode of civilization, which traps us in what author Graham Hancock calls the "alert, problem-solving state of mind." Our separation from nature is widely appreciated; less understood is our separation from a profound alternate state of consciousness to which our ancestors turned regularly for information and guidance.

Our being cut off from this altered state benefits corporations, which need obedient workers toiling inside what Timothy Leary called *air-conditioned anthills*. They prefer their staff and customers to not access subversive truths. There's a whole library of Alexandria waiting for us to browse, but we fail to access it because of our cultural conditioning.

The price for this disassociation from Source has been tragic, not only for self-alienated people riding the ghost-train of late-stage capitalism, but for all the Earth's animals and ecosystems. Our avarice, our narcissism — what indigenous people call *wetiko* — is killing the planet in an orgy of resource depletion, climate change, pollution and ocean acidification.

And for what? So a small oligarchy can earn more billions of dollars than they could ever spend? So we can drive our climate-controlled SUVs to the climate-controlled shopping mall?

It's absurd! And the fossil fuels will be gone in a few decades anyway. Most of us know this, but we're not sure what to do. Some are working on technical solutions to environmental problems. Others are workshopping new economic and political systems to get us past the fruitless "left versus right" debate, and whether the solution is more government control (socialism) or less (libertarianism).

Yet something crucial is missing, without which our culture, economy and ecosystems will collapse. We'll be like passengers rearranging the deck chairs on the Titanic, hitting the iceberg of ecological collapse even as we fret about which plastic containers go in the recycling bin.

What is that *missing something*?

It's the heart-felt recognition that *nature is sacred*. And that we, as part of nature, *are also sacred*.

And that's where the teacher plants come in. For they are the red pill in *Matrix* terms that awakens us to the other dimensions and nature's secret teachings.

That *nature is sacred* is something the teacher plants communicate, over and over. And they convey this teaching not as an arid intellectual idea, but as a truth that hits you so hard in the solar plexus you may be left gasping for air, bent over crying, or even vomiting.

So here I am, several years into this long strange journey, a sort of Morpheus ready to share with others the details of my first twelve ayahuasca ceremonies in what I've come to think of as the Year of Drinking Magic.

I know that not everyone will consume ayahuasca or other entheogenic plants. But according to the hundredth monkey syndrome, not everyone needs to. And there are other modalities of awakening that don't require visionary plants. I don't know if the number is one in a hundred or one in a thousand, but there is some threshold, some tipping point, beyond which if enough people shift their consciousness, the consciousness of the whole human species will move.

And hopefully in time. What we do in the next ten or twenty years will arguably be more important than anything we do in the next ten thousand.

We need to turn the juggernaut around *that quickly*.

Why do you go away? So that you can come back. So that you can see the place you came from with new eyes and extra colors. And the people there see you differently, too. Coming back to where you started is not the same as never leaving.

— TERRY PRATCHETT, *A Hat Full of Sky*

In December 2013 I travelled to Iquitos, Peru to trek in the Amazon rainforest and participate in shamanic ceremonies at a nearby retreat center. At the time of this 10-day trip, ayahuasca — the visionary tea used as a diagnostic tool by local *curanderos* (healers) — was entering the consciousness of the cultural mainstream in a big way.

Nowadays there's no end of writing about ayahuasca, and websites like Reset.me (for which I've written) offer many accounts of people's experiences and healing. But before 2013 less was written about it, at least in books, magazines or popular websites.

I'd researched ayahuasca casually for several years and recall there being a dearth of good information. With the odd exception, most easily obtained online accounts of ayahuasca were short and sketchy, and often amateurishly written.

I found myself anxious to know everything possible about how the medicine *felt*. And what did people *see*?

In the late 2000s I met a woman who'd drunk it and had an interesting story to tell, but it was short. She'd encountered herself in what felt like a recent past life, and she said something about seeing "colors" and "geometry."

It was unsatisfying.

I eventually found my way to some useful books.

One was Jeremy Narby's excellent *The Cosmic Serpent: DNA and the Origins of Knowledge* that explained ayahuasca at the crux of science and speculation. And there was Terence McKenna's spellbinding book *True Hallucinations: Being an Account of the Author's Extraordinary Adventures in the Devil's Paradise*, which — while it starts out as an account of a trip in search of the ayahuasca vine — ends up being more a tale about his and his brother Dennis's transformative experiences with psychedelic mushrooms. (It remains a favorite of mine, especially in the audio-recording format that McKenna taped himself, replete with sound effects.)

Another useful book I encountered was Charles Hayes' *Tripping: An Anthology of True-Life Psychedelic Adventures*, which offers first-hand accounts from dozens of people of their experiences in a variety of altered states from a range of psychedelics.

While most of the accounts are positive and often deeply spiritual, the book also contains cautionary tales of "bad trips" that usually resulted from a poor "set and setting" or over-consumption of a particular psychedelic (often by an inexperienced user). Useful as those accounts are, the book mostly records people's "trips" on LSD and other drugs that were popular in the 1970s. (The author's introduction is a wonderful treatise on psychedelics that's worth the price of the book in itself.)

Poet William S. Burroughs had found ayahuasca in the 1960s, but it hadn't entered the popular imagination in those heady counterculture times. So I was pleased to discover Steven Beyer's *Singing to the Plants: A Guide to Mestizo Shamanism in the Upper Amazon*, which is an excellent anthropological account of the shamanic practices and the role of ayahuasca in local culture in that part of the world.

If Beyer's book placed me like a football on the kickstand of curiosity, it was Graham Hancock's aforementioned *Supernatural: Meetings with the Ancient Teachers of Mankind* that punted me through the goal posts of psychedelic commitment.

I concluded that, whatever truth or illusion lay ahead of me, I simply couldn't go through this life without at least once consuming one of these sacred plants that had been so influential throughout human history. There were other reasons, but this was *reason enough*.

* * *

In 2013 I worked as editor of a couple of trade magazines concerned with pollution prevention and municipal recycling. The 25th anniversary of my career in that business was approaching and I felt inspired to do something special to commemorate the occasion.

I hadn't traveled anywhere unusual for years — typically taking my kids on ski trips and other family holidays. Once in a while I'd escape the chilly Canadian winters with a last-minute deal to a Caribbean resort. The idea grew on me that I should step outside my comfort zone and visit the Amazon rainforest — the Mecca of environmentalists. I'd been writing about the environment for decades, but hadn't spent much time in it!

I browsed travel websites in search of a suitable tour. I wanted a Lonely Planet kind of trip. I also wanted to drink ayahuasca and, while there were websites for retreat centers, I wasn't sure which one to choose.

One day I stumbled upon a short internet video from a company called Pulse Tours, based in Canada. It showed people trekking in the jungle and visiting an island to feed different kinds of monkeys that clambered aboard a motorized canoe. As I explored the site further, I learned the tours also included ayahuasca ceremonies. After a few emails (the owner was guiding a group in the jungle) I signed on.

Once I committed to the trip, some interesting things happened.

I'd listened to a talk from the late Terence McKenna on YouTube in which McKenna outlined his ideas of time flowing both forward and backward, with events not simply pushed forward by the past, but pulled into the future by an unseen *attractor*. This attractor is the *eschaton*, or the *transcendental object at the end of time*.

Time, McKenna said, doesn't flow linearly, but more like a spiral that speeds up into a concrescence.

After booking my trip to Peru, I felt as though somehow the experience I was *yet to have* drinking ayahuasca was flowing back through time, like an echo from the future. My priorities shifted; I felt some sort of healing underway; I noticed that things that used to make me anxious, and certain compulsions, began to fade. I drank less alcohol, for example, to the extent that a month before the trip I drank nothing at all. I thought of sex from time to time, but not obsessively. (I had no girlfriend at the time, which helped.)

This was a useful development, as the info Pulse Tours sent me about preparation for the trip included observation of a *dieta*. The dieta required no alcohol, no sex, no pork, no salt, no spicy food, and a few other restrictions. It's a South American protocol before drinking ayahuasca. While some of it may simply be traditional, scientists note that the restrictions prepare the brain's neurotransmitters to accept the dimethyltryptamine (DMT) in the psychedelic brew.

Tourists may observe the dieta for as little as a week before ceremony, or even just a couple of days. I drifted into observing it for a full month.

Strangest of all was the feeling whenever I strolled in nature, even just when walking the dog, that the plants and trees were quietly communicating with me. It sounds crazy, but if I'm to faithfully record my experience, I must confess that I truly sensed communion with the plants and bushes and trees around me, as if the denizens of the vegetative kingdom somehow knew of my impending trip and were telepathically reaching out, engaging. I wondered whether if somehow — through the mycelia and spores or even some morphogenic plant consciousness – the vegetative kingdom could communicate from where I lived in Ontario all the way down to the Amazon basin.

With the backwash of time, I wondered if my about-to-be-increased sensitivity to plant intelligence was elevating. In any case, plants and trees no long felt like inanimate objects as I passed them on foot; they were intelligent life forms that interact with and influence us.

* * *

My flight to Iquitos was uneventful.

I departed Toronto in the afternoon and switched planes near New York. The contrast was striking between the security and searches I endured in my four-hour stay in the Newark airport compared to the far more relaxed protocols in Lima, Peru, where I again changed planes — this time from an intercontinental aircraft to a small regional jet. I realized that Peru simply isn't part of the whole "War on Terror" narrative and supposed threats from the Muslim world. Airport security there was like a trip back to the United States of the 1960s, with only cursory inspection of bags and identification (most of the time).

During the flight I reflected back on my only previous experience with psychedelic substances, which occurred in the mid-1980s on a camping trip in the Adirondack Mountains with an American cousin. It involved LSD.

I hiked with him and a childhood friend of his for a couple of days deep into the mountain range, combating rain storms and traversing fields of slippery boulders. Being from Ontario, I was more used to paddling a canoe with the occasional portage breaking up the trip. This adventure was nothing but a long portage!

Late one afternoon we arrived at the shores of a mountain lake in the middle of a tremendous rain and set up a makeshift camp. When the rain subsided we cooked up some ramen noodles over a campfire, and my cousin announced he'd brought along some LSD. He produced a small amount of blotter acid folded neatly inside a piece of aluminum foil.

Trepidatiously I agreed to try the hallucinogen the following afternoon. After swallowing the LSD tab I sat on a flat rock overlooking the lake, which was about a kilometer or two across, maybe further. I eventually saw the *fractal geometry* of the ripples. There was a complex, repeating pattern in nature, and I could comprehend the geometry of the wind on the waves, as though I was watching *how something is done*.

Initially I didn't think I was feeling the drug's effects, but it occurred to me I wouldn't normally sit and stare at the surface of a lake for hours and hours.

"So this is what LSD feels like," I thought to myself.

Then my attention shifted to my sense of hearing. I developed super-hearing and could hear every single insect and bird in the forest for miles, not as a cacophony but each one — thousands and thousands — isolated by super-attenuation. It was amazing! My sense of reality shifted; I'd never considered that my ordinary state of mind filtered out so much information, presumably to make it easy to navigate ordinary reality.

Perhaps, I speculated, hunter-gatherers hear more like this, not having been trained to shut out so much of the natural world.

The next morning my cousin and his friend asked about my LSD trip as we huddled over the stove and made a light breakfast of instant oatmeal. I told them about it and about my super-hearing. They appeared to believe me, but challenged me to prove it. I mentioned I'd heard a very distinct sound emanating from the far side of the lake. It sounded like water coming out of a pipe, falling about half a meter and splashing on smooth stone.

"Let's go find it!" I said.

After we broke camp and shouldered our heavy packs, we set off to look for the spot I'd described. After an hour or more of hiking I led them to it. Beyond some jungly overgrowth there, coming out of the mountain at about waist height, was a small green copper pipe that seemed almost ancient. It produced a steady stream of cold mountain water that spilled onto a smooth rock below, making exactly the sound I'd heard the day before.

* * *

The regional aircraft landed in Iquitos and I was struck immediately by the small size of the landing strip and the ominous presence of the encroaching jungle. Abandoned aircraft and disused vehicles littered the edge of the fenced area.

At the baggage carousel I met several of the other Canadians who were to accompany me on the 10-day excursion (to which I'd added a couple of extra days at the end, for recovery and transition).

These were three men in their twenties who all knew one another from growing up in Strathroy, Ontario: Michael (Mike) Sanders, Carl Erik, and Sydney (Sid) Smith. All three were fit and brimming with humor. Carl is a bodybuilder and Michael an athlete who can perform handstands. It felt like I had personal bodyguards as we exited the building and found a mototaxi to transport us to our hotel.

We were joined in the lobby of the Golden Star hotel by Pulse Tours owner Dan Cleland, a quick-witted guy who looks vaguely like Jon Hamm of *Mad Men* television fame, and his equally attractive Russian-Canadian girlfriend Tatyana. Cleland also grew up in Strathroy and is friends with Mike, Carl and Erik, so we had ourselves a fun and familiar group from the get-go.

Rounding out the guests was John ("Jun Jun"), a handsome mixed-race dude originally from the Philippines who lived in Florida and ended up as my roommate on the trip. (The other person was our jungle guide Victor Naro, who we wouldn't meet until after our stay in the riverine city.)

Cleland introduced everyone and gave us a quick orientation in the small sitting room of the hotel. We'd spend a day sightseeing in Iquitos, then head by mototaxi to the nearby port town of Nauta and travel by boat on a tributary river to the Amazon itself, and on to a rustic resort near the riverside village of Libertad. We'd spend three days there trekking through the forest and taking boat trips to different points of interest. We'd then travel by boat and mototaxi to a spiritual center where we'd drink ayahuasca with curanderos. We'd be offered three nighttime ceremonies over four days.

Jun Jun and I each had our own rooms in Iquitos, though we'd pair up for the rest of the trip. Dan and Tatyana had their own digs, and the three lads from Strathroy shared a suite. I recall enjoying my solitary room, with its tile floors and walls, and the bed set up with starched white sheets. It felt very Spanish. Very colonial.

I went for a short walk that night on streets that hummed with mototaxis. Signs on posts warned tourists of long jail sentences for soliciting sex with minors.

In our brief stay in Iquitos our group bonded over some short excursions and meals at a couple of interesting restaurants, including one that floated out on the river.

Iquitos itself is a fascinating place. Only a few decades ago it was a small port town, but the population has exploded in recent years to somewhere around 370,000 people. It's the largest city in the world not connected to the outside by a road (one can only get there by plane or boat.) Because of the expense in hauling cars there by river, most people get around on motorcycles or mototaxis (a kind of motorcycle-powered rickshaw).

The roads are not for the faint of heart; traffic moves like a chase scene from a *Mad Max* movie. It's not uncommon to see whole families clinging to one another on a single motorcycle, babies in their mothers' laps.

Everyone seemed to agree the main highlight was the Belen market — a hodgepodge of shops and stalls that sprawls over many square kilometers of canopied alleyways and open-air spaces. In addition to all kinds of fruit and vegetables and conventional meats, one might witness a large jungle rat being butchered, or some strange glistening aquatic creature. We laughed at the many stalls of homemade lotions and potions, quite a few of which were for male potency, with memorable titles like "All Night Long."

Before we had time to grow restless we left Iquitos by mototaxi for Nauta, stopping along the way to enjoy a meal at a roadside cafe that set a new standard in "rustic." Jungle rat was on the menu.

In Nauta our backpacks and other luggage were passed down the steep red mudbank of the wide Marañón River (a major Amazon tributary) and loaded into a commodious motorboat with a canopy-covered cabin.

We set off under a warm cerulean sky for the tiny village of Libertad, several hours away. Dense jungle bordered the wide serpentine river, and in the distance we periodically spotted some of the blind dolphins that ply those waters, their skin pink from the color of their prey.

The pilot idled the boat in the middle of the river at the place where the tributary mixes with the different-colored muddy water of the Amazon. We went for a short swim off the side of the boat, and were warned against swimming near the river bank.

That's where the caymans and piraña hang out, the captain said.

The water was so dense with red silt that visibility was zero beneath the surface.

I recall being the only one who lacked the upper body strength to pull himself back into the boat, the gunnels of which were high above the water. This reminded me that I was older than the rest of the gang, with whom I otherwise interacted as a peer. Bruises appeared on my stomach the next day from being dragged over the wooden edge by the younger men.

Later that afternoon we arrived at our jungle lodge in Libertad and went to our different rooms. The lodge — which has since been replaced or augmented by Cleland with a much-upgraded larger facility called the Arkana Spiritual Center — was very basic. It was comprised of thatch huts, each of which contained platform beds covered by mosquito netting. Each structure sat on stilts to endure the rainy season, when the river rises and water laps the bottom of the doorframes, or even floods whole rooms. (The open grassy areas where we walked are navigated by canoe at those times.)

Jun Jun and I paired up in one stilt-hut, whose most distinctive feature was the presence of a spider roughly the size of a dinner plate that hung out on the window pane about a meter from my bed. He remained there the whole three days of our stay. I never saw the spider directly — only its outline beneath a thin piece of fabric that served as a makeshift curtain — but it was definitely on the *inside* of the window. It didn't have the shape of a tarantula (which live up in the thatch and can be heard scuttling around at night): it had long skeletal legs and a smooth body.

A lifelong arachnophobe, I endured this neighbor because there was no point removing it. There was a two-inch gap between the floor and the bottom of the door, so these sorts of creatures came and went as they pleased. I slept well at night as long as I was under the mosquito net, which I carefully tucked under the mattress on all four sides. (It creeped me out to even tuck in the fabric. What if something was already hiding in there?)

Our stay at Libertad was brief but intense. The guides took us on three excursions per day (one each morning, afternoon and night). We trekked the jungle on foot — at night with headlamps — at locations near the lodge and also far away by boat. Highlights included swinging Tarzan-style from a long rope set up in the jungle, a visit to "Monkey Island," and my feet getting stung repeatedly by tiny fire ants one time when I jumped onto the riverbank to pee wearing only flip flops (a mistake I didn't repeat).

Interestingly, the day we visited Monkey Island the monkeys wouldn't accept food. It was the day each month they instinctively eat only fiber from reeds, to rid their digestive systems of parasites. That this occurred across the different species of monkeys was striking, and consistent with scientist Rupert Sheldrake's idea of morphogenic fields.

I recall us felling a whole tree with a machete to harvest the "heart of palm" near the top, and our being intrigued by a very long column of cutter ants that carried leaves to an enormous anthill almost two meters high and about as wide as a swimming pool. (Strangely, our jungle guide Victor was very blasé about these interesting ants, perhaps from familiarity, as I tend to be about squirrels in the municipal parks of Toronto.)

Night treks were the spookiest. It was not uncommon to have close encounters with black scorpions on twigs and leaves (sometimes at eye level). Tarantulas and other spiders were ubiquitous, as well as venomous snakes. Tall rubber boots made me feel only a bit better about the risk of stepping on something.

I was offered the chance to skip one of the excursions and just lounge around the lodge, but by the second day of trekking our group had bonded like an army platoon and I didn't want to let my comrades down by sitting anything out. In fact, I eventually called our group the Ayahuasca Test Pilots, based on a sign painted on the back of a mototaxi. (Brotherhood of the Screaming Abyss would also have been good too, referring to the title of ethnobotanist Dennis McKenna's book about his life and growing up with famous brother Terence.)

The most fun and unusual event (and one that really brought our team together) was traveling by boat to a small Amazon village to play an impromptu soccer match against our South American guides. (They won after Sid, whose idea this all was, injured his toe and I had to take his place. The match suddenly went from four points each to 8-5 for the locals.) I'll never forget the smiles and laughter of the guides, who apparently had never played soccer with clients before. Their prize was a case of beer.

I found myself easily winded running around during the soccer match. My poor physical condition related to my having spent much of the previous year sitting around on the couch, recovering from a broken leg after falling on ice while snowboarding in Whistler, BC.

Eventually the jungle trekking segment of the tour concluded and we parted ways from Victor and his assistant with some sadness. We made our way by boat back to the port of Nauta, and then by mototaxi on to the ayahuasca retreat center.

This rural mototaxi trip was especially hair-raising. In addition to having to get out and help push the vehicles through red mud (it had rained recently), we crossed a bridge whose surface was missing most of its wooden planks. Above a raging river, the driver was only able to cross by lining up the three wheels of the vehicle with the few remaining planks. A margin of error of only a few inches separated us from plunging onto the rocks and water below — a peril that didn't persuade our driver to slow down.

So it was a relief to me when we encountered the street sign pointing us toward the Nihue Rao Spiritual Center. We passed through the gate, which was manned by armed guards, grabbed our backpacks from the rear of the mototaxis, and were directed to our rooms in the facility.

From this place, Jung said, "the approach to the numinous is the real therapy"; the real healing of old wounds that frees us up to feel how every thing, every one is calling to us. Imbued with its own rhizomatic, instinctive intelligence, ensouled and dreaming us open, everything wants to ravish us alive.

— MELISSA LA FLAMME, *Opening to Mystery*

We can hardly bear to look. The shadow may carry the best of the life we have not lived. Go into the basement, the attic, the refuse bin. Find gold there. Find an animal who has not been fed or watered. It is you! This neglected, exiled animal, hungry for attention, is part of your self.

— MARION WOODMAN
(as quoted by Stephen Cope in
The Great Work of Your Life)

Nihue Rao is a version of jungle lodge that's become fairly standard due to increased ayahuasca tourism on the new Gringo Trail. A variety of thatched-roof buildings sprawl across a sandy clearing in the forest. A generator hums to life for a few hours each day to provide electricity for lights and recharging of cell phones and cameras. A small coterie of *mestizo* (mixed race) staff attend to the groundskeeping, preparing simple "ayahuasca diet" food in the kitchen (i.e., no salt, no pork or red meat, no spices, no alcohol, etc.). A few men patrol the perimeter with shotguns: roaming security.

The most important building at Nihue Rao is the maloka (ceremonial building) where ayahuasca ceremonies are conducted. The structure is tall and round with an enormous Polynesian-style thatch roof. Inside, thin mattresses are spaced around the outer edge of the circular wood floor, each with pillows at one end and a plastic "purge bucket" set to the side. The mattresses for visitors are on one side of the maloka, with several mattresses on the other side reserved for the curanderos and their assistants. Some shamanic tools sit on the floor in that area, including the *shacapa* (a leaf-bundle rattle) and the *maraca* (a seed-filled gourd rattle). These rhythmic implements are the most important tools among Amazonian shamans, serving the same purpose as the shaman's drum in other traditions.

Other paraphernalia include fabrics woven with colorful Shipibo designs and containers for serving the psychotropic brew, though these are normally set up just before ceremony.

Near the maloka there's a building with washroom stalls on one side and showers on the other, with open-air sinks. Just beyond this building there's a barrack-style facility where guests stay, two to a room; each room contains beds with mosquito netting and a comfortable hammock in the center for lounging.

Though the accommodations are basic, they're light-filled and clean, and for the most part — unlike the jungle lodge — the spiders seem to reside *outside* the rooms.

Nihue Rao also boasts a large house for the lead shaman and his family, a building that holds the big kitchen with connecting dining hall, another with a communal room with couches and board games, an "art maloka" with easels, paper and art supplies, and some private cabins for people staying for extended retreats and dietas.

Notable among the animals at Nihue Rao during my stay was a baby spider monkey that wrapped its long arms around the boot of its owner (one of the staff) and a number of colorful parrots, one of whom had been trained to sing dramatic opera arias. I was astonished at the bird's vocabulary and vocal range! Unfortunately this bird also made a habit of attacking me from the air, like a scene from Alfred Hitchcock's film *The Birds*. On several occasions I had to bat it away forcefully as it raged at me with its talons and beak — a comeuppance perhaps for my indifference to opera.

Nihue Rao is comfortable enough but not a place North American or European travellers would normally seek out, except that in such jungle lodges the desired experience doesn't belong to this dimension. This is the setting for trips into *hyperspace* or what the locals call *el mundo espiritual*. This is a place not to just think about God or the Gaian Oversoul, but to meet her in person, ask questions directly, and maybe have your ass handed to you in the process, as she defrags your mind and body (to paraphrase psychonaut Rak Razam). You don't have to read a three-thousand-year-old account about someone in the Levant seeing a burning bush or climbing a magic ladder; you can see and climb yourself.

CEREMONY ONE

Shortly after our arrival at Nihue Rao our group was introduced to Rapha (Raphael) and Anna — two assistant curanderos who were apprenticing under the lead curandero, Ricardo Amaringo. Rapha was a young man with dreads, a beard, and yogi attire who hailed from the United States but who was fluent in Spanish, having lived in Argentina as a child. Anna was a young Portuguese woman with excellent English and a penchant for wearing billowy cotton pants decorated with snakes and Shipibo designs.

They told us some of the regular curanderos and staff at Nihue Rao were away for the holidays (this being the week of New Year's Eve) but that lead curandero Amaringo was traveling back specially to host our three upcoming ceremonies, which would be conducted over four days. We were to drink on the second night of our stay, have one night off, and then drink two nights in a row. Amaringo, we were warned, was on the tail end of a long plant dieta and might be groggy. Amaringo's sister Ersilia and a gentleman named Erjomenes (the Spanish version of Geronimo) would also sit with us as curanderos and sing in ceremony. Each of us received a photocopied information sheet about how to prepare for ayahuasca ceremony, and spent the first day of our arrival lounging around and exploring the property. A couple of the guys went for a swim in a nearby river, and complained about emerging covered with what I surmised was oil from a small slick.

Most of the gang turned over their dirty clothes to be laundered, but I elected to wash mine myself in the sinks at the shower facility, which was well provisioned with big bricks of yellow laundry soap. (This turned out to be a good decision, as my clothes were dry on the line later that day; the others didn't get their clothes back until the end of the week.)

I lay in the hammock in my room while Jun Jun took a long nap. I read the handout about ceremony. In addition to the recommendations to avoid eating after about noon on the day of ceremony and to wear comfortable clothes, etc., I noticed the offer (a recommendation really) that people consume a "vomitive medicine" the day before ceremony, to clear out their digestive systems.

Along with the rest of the group, I declined this suggestion. Our group leader Dan Cleland had had a bad experience with it, or at least his dad did. Cleland had brought his father and one of his dad's friends down to Peru to drink ayahuasca, and both men had used the "vomitive medicine" as directed and spent the whole day throwing up and feeling terrible. The experience so turned them off they never drank the sacred brew at all. I later learned the medicine is a liquid latex harvested from local trees. I elected to trust that my own digestive tract was extremely clean already, as I'd observed the ayahuasca diet for a full month before arriving in Peru.

I felt restless that first day and night at the retreat center. It was like being a soldier the night before the D-Day invasion; my mind was preoccupied with the impending launch into the unknown...

Finally the big day came. Nothing stands out as particularly interesting from the day itself. I tried to nap as much as I could, but I was too filled with anticipation to sleep. I had an average-size vegetarian meal for lunch, and then ate and drank nothing except some water and an apple that I consumed at about 4:00 pm. (Ayahuasca is imbibed on an empty stomach.)

Around that time, along with the other participants, I took a "flower shower." This consisted of pouring flower-saturated water over myself from a bucket in an outdoor shower stall. We were instructed to let the water dry from our bodies without toweling and to allow any leaves or petals to remain on our skin. We performed this ritual behind a small building at the back of the property near the open pit where the ayahuasca is brewed. The ritual is meant to cleanse the body and also make it more fragrant, so as to appeal to the plant spirit.

After our showers, we walked over to the main *maloca* where Rapha and Anna sat across from us and described the protocols for the night ahead.

We each took turns sitting on a large mattress in front of them, and were asked what our *intention* would be for that evening's ceremony. This would later be conveyed to the shamans who would help us with their *icaros* (medicine songs).

We were told that intentions could be as simple as, say, "cleansing" or more complex, such as, "I wish to overcome the fear that's blocking further success in my career."

I told Rapha and Anna I wouldn't set a specific intention for this — my first ayahuasca ceremony — and would instead simply approach the experience with openness to whatever the plant wished to show me. It was like a first date.

Rapha seemed to think this was a good idea. We agreed that I could set more specific intentions for the second and third ceremony. I returned to my mat, my mind reviewing concerns about vomiting and diarrhea, which often occur when ayahuasca purges the body of its various blockages, both physical and energetic.

Ayahuasca may have originally been used hundreds or thousands of years ago as an emetic, to rid the body of the intestinal parasites that concern jungle dwellers. The plant's psychotropic properties may have been discovered by chance when someone mashed up the vine together with *chacruna* leaves or some other DMT-rich plant. Curanderos say the plant spirits themselves gave their ancestors these instructions.

Whether by trial and error or by mystical instruction, the brew we call ayahuasca (and sometimes *yagé*) is simply a strategy to allow the bloodstream to uptake dimethyltryptamine (DMT) that would normally be blocked by chemicals in the digestive system. The vine acts as a monoamine oxidase inhibitor (MAOI) and the companion plant provides the psychoactive DMT.

Recipes for ayahuasca vary. The brew always includes the ayahuasca vine (*Banisteriopsis caapi*) and another DMT-rich plant. In Peru the companion plant is normally chacruna (*Psychotria viridis*), but in Brazil, Ecuador and Columbia chagropanga (the Quechua name for *Diplopterys cabrerana*) may be used.

Complicating matters, Brazil has evolved and exported a whole other style of ayahuasca consumption, that being the tea of the Santo Daime church. The brew itself is highly similar to that of other ayahuasca traditions, but instead of sitting at night with curanderos, drinkers of daime normally hold their ceremonies during the day or evening; there is no *shaman* and instead everyone stands on their feet engaged in a formal dance much of the time, with men and women separated in rows on opposite sides of a table altar. Santo Daime is a syncretic religion, fusing elements of Christianity, African mysticism and Amazonian shamanism. Portuguese hymns are sung in unison from hymn books, with emphasis on Catholic saints and symbolism.

Another variation from Brazil is the União do Vegetal (UDV), which is recognized as a church in the United States' legal system. Adherents of União do Vegetal (union of the plants) call their version of the sacred tea *hoasca*.

Some researchers support the notion that DMT-bearing ayahuasca-like brews were used in other times and other cultures, including the lands that gave rise to the Abrahamic religions. The bark of the Acacia tree contains DMT and is found across the Middle East. The *Acacia Nilotica* is depicted, rather tellingly, in Egyptian wall paintings as the Tree of Life. The significance of a serpent giving Adam and Eve the knowledge of good and evil from the apple of a tree will not be lost on ayahuasca acolytes.

Interestingly, a concept of the spine containing light energy analogous to that of yoga traditions and kundalini energy is recorded in the Pyramid Texts — among the world's oldest sacred texts. Some believe naturally occurring DMT is held in the spine, and that yoga is a technique for releasing large amounts into the brain. The ancients may have accessed ayahuasca-like experiences not via plants, but by mastering the flow of their bodies' endogenous DMT.

* * *

After all seven of us set our intentions with Rapha and Anna, we were free to leave the *maloca* and rest in our *tambos* (rooms) or otherwise pass the time until ceremony. I rested for a while in the hammock and drank a cup of very weak tea.

At about 7:30 pm I changed into a thick white cotton shirt and pants, both decorated with bright Shipibo designs, that I'd picked up in the Belen market in Iquitos specifically to wear in ceremony.

I returned to the *maloca* and lay on my mat, my back and shoulders leaning on some pillows piled up against the building's curved inner wall.

As other participants trailed in and took up positions on their mats, I looked up at the enormous round inner vault of the *maloca* and the wagon wheel beam structures at the top that held it together. They looked distinctly like a giant spider web.

I was filled with apprehension. How to describe such a feeling...

It was like sitting in a roller coaster car as it climbs the steep initial hill... *clickity clack, clickity clack*... my heart beating in anticipation.

As night fell, just before 8:00 pm, and with little fanfare, the curanderos entered the building.

Ricardo Amaringo sat directly across from us, with one other curandero on each side.

Amaringo is a fairly small mestizo man with tan skin and jet black hair; he dresses unassumingly in T-shirts and shorts. He's the very opposite of a showman seeking any kind of attention. In another context he might be the guy who takes your keys at the airport parking lot, or who works the bar at a golf club. Yet this man is a master of inter-dimensional reality, as I was about to discover.

Trained in the Shipibo tradition, I was later told, Amaringo has been a curandero for more than 20 years and regularly practices dietas with different plants. In fact, he had just finished a long dieta with one plant from which he was still drowsy when he arrived back at the center.

On Amaringo's right sat Erjomenes (pronounced er-hom-eh-ness, though many defaulted to the Anglicized Geronimo) — an elderly man with high-cheekboned features. Erjomenes fit my mental picture of the Inca wise man and I was happy when he was assigned to sing me a personal *icaro* during each of the three ceremonies.

On Amaringo's left sat Ersilia, Amaringo's sister — a strong curandero in her own right. Ersilia is a very warm and kind person who smiled and spontaneously hugged me when we first met. She felt instantly familiar to me, like a favorite aunt. Ersilia also makes crafts in the Shipibo style such as brightly colored bead bracelets, ornamental blankets, necklaces and other jewelry. She spent many hours on the property during the day displaying these wares, some of which I bought before my departure.

Rapha and Anna sat to the far right of the curanderos. They would drink a very small serving of *la medicina* so as to be with us in spirit but remain sober enough to help manage the ceremony's practical aspects.

We were joined this evening by another guest — Geoffrey — a middle-aged seeker from Baltimore on a month-long retreat.

In time Amaringo started serving the ayahuasca tea to participants, each of whom approached and sat down on a blanket directly in front of Amaringo's mattress. The shaman poured the thick brew into a small clear glass from a ceramic jug, and wiped off the edge after each person drank in a way that reminded me of communion wine in church. Some participants paused or whispered a prayer while kneeling with their cup, before tossing back the liquid.

I was the last to drink. The ayahuasca liquid lived up to its reputation as a repulsive elixir. The taste reminded me vaguely of prune juice, perhaps with an admixture of burnt coffee. The flavor didn't bother me as much as the sticky texture. I gagged reflexively when it hit my empty stomach.

Returning to my mattress, I reflected that there was no going back now; the psychedelic brew I'd read about for years was inside my body, and all I could do was await its effects.

Ah, such difference there is between an *experience* and a mere *idea!*

I lay on my mat, taking some comfort in the knowledge that this particular concoction was not adulterated with additives like the powerful hallucinogenic plant Toé. I'd asked about this early in the day. Toé is a plant suited only for very experienced shamans. Its visions can be nightmarish and can last for days. Some retreat centers are rumored to add it to the ayahuasca brew to guarantee gringo tourists their much-sought visions.

I had no watch, but started to estimate the minutes passing.

The shamans drank the medicine and everyone sat in silence. The electric lights remained on for about ten minutes. At some point Anna got up and turned them off from a switch near the main door. We remained quiet with just a candle for light for another ten minutes or so. Then this was extinguished and we all rested silently in the *maloca*.

In time the noisy generator shut down in the distance, and soft jungle sounds filled the night air. The fading light of evening silhouetted the dark jungle, visible through the large screen windows that ran the circumference of the building. Distant lightning occasionally lit up the space: we would have a large rainstorm that night.

Music pulsed from a nearby village: it was New Year's Eve and the faint sounds of revelers and their stereos were the only distraction in the otherwise pristine setting.

After what felt like 30 to 40 minutes I began to feel the effects of the medicine. Warmth spread from my stomach throughout my body and extremities. I sat up as a dizzying rush pervaded me.

Oh boy, I thought. *Here we go.*

* * *

As I assumed a seated position, a brilliant geometric pattern gradually filled the center of my vision. It's difficult to describe and no words can ever do it justice. What unfolded in front of me was a pattern that became the standard fare for the beginning of each of my next few ayahuasca journeys.

How to even *suggest* what was before me?

Imagine a black background with a linear pattern superimposed on it. The pattern is somewhat like the weaving of a basket, but larger. The lines are made up of brilliant color. The color started as a deep red, but soon grew in brilliance and pulsed into green and red, then blue or purple or mauve, with orange accents. These were not the colors from a painter's box; instead they were neon bright, like the lasers used in theater productions or rock music concerts.

There was nothing uncertain about the design. This was not some vague dream. The geometry was crystal clear, exact, and the thin outlines of each component of the design were razor thin and completely uniform. A computer couldn't do a better job rendering each shape with great precision. The outlined shapes initially looked flat, two-dimensional, and covered my entire visual field. I noticed they remained exactly the same and vivid whether my eyes were open or closed. When my eyes were open, the geometry was superimposed on the dark shapes of the *maloca* in the background.

This was *hyperspace* — the other dimension of reality or consciousness referred to by psychedelic writers. I was seeing it, and it was *real*. No matter where I looked, the pattern maintained its integrity in every detail.

My imagination simply could not make this up, I thought to myself again and again. Months later I would hear Terence McKenna talk in one of his famous recordings about the main risk from DMT not being chemical overdose, but rather *death by astonishment*.

And astonished I was.

As the first icaro began, the geometric pattern grew in intensity and began pulsing. Over time the pattern became more complex and three-dimensional. The shapes had a decidedly Haida or Navaho flair.

Now I understand where those designs on pottery and blankets come from, I thought to myself.

Next, the whole thing began moving. As the icaros developed in intensity so did the pattern and vision. I began to see that I could travel into the pattern, which was now very three-dimensional, with my consciousness *flying* into it or out, at will. It was a bit like the perspective of Luke Skywalker attacking the Death Star in *Star Wars*: he flies over the Death Star's exterior, then down into the crevices and valleys of its exterior pattern. My point of view was like that, looking at the pattern from outside, then traveling into it.

As I moved around and inside the pattern, I realized I was learning to *navigate*. A thought occurred to me: that the geometric designs on Shipibo blankets and other crafts were not simply *designs*; they were *maps*.

This went on for some time, perhaps an hour.

Once in a while I'd check myself. Could I return to ordinary reality? I was pleasantly surprised to find the answer was "yes." I simply had to turn my attention to the physical objects around me and I was perfectly grounded in the regular world.

Well, perhaps not *perfectly*...

In the darkness to my left I could feel my water bottle, my flashlight, a roll of toilet paper, and my shoulder bag. I could focus on the *maloca* and the dim outlines of the trees outside the building, dark against the night sky that occasionally flashed with lightning. Simply put, I could *toggle* between the psychedelic dimension and the realm of ordinary reality. With the knowledge that I was in no danger, I worked at staying in the psychedelic reality as much as possible, pushing further and further into it, wondering what secrets it held.

I noticed two things as the ceremony continued. First (and thankfully!) I never stopped *being me*. My core consciousness never went away and the little inner voice that I associate with *me* — which I came to think of as my ego — never dissipated completely. But I will say that the ego voice held a less commanding position in the schemata that unfolded. My egoic voice was like a friendly familiar companion, along for the ride, chatting away and taking it all in with as much surprise and elation as the deeper part of my consciousness, my true *self*.

Second, I noticed the importance of the icaros. How on earth, I wondered, would anyone get anything from ayahuasca without those songs? It was evident that the shamans were literally singing this spirit world into existence, like the aborigines of Australia and their song lines.

When the songs grew in tempo and intensity, the visions grew in strength and complexity. When they subsided, the visions began to fade, and tapered off completely when the songs ended.

How can one describe an icaro?

I hesitate to try, but they are strange and powerful, otherworldly and at times astonishingly beautiful, lyrical, sweet and sad. Just as I learned to visually fly into the geometric patterns, I learned to ride the waves of the songs. The more I paid attention to the icaros (which we'd been told to do) the more structure the visions held, the more purposive everything felt that was being presented.

With eyes open at some points the laser-like brightly-colored outlines disappeared entirely and my visual field was filled with a pattern that looked like it had been carefully carved from panes of frosted glass; it was semi-transparent and maintained its "design integrity" in every respect.

I played games with the designs, trying to find flaws in them. I'd look at one spot, look away, then look back quickly to the same place. It would be there, solid and real, just as a building in ordinary reality would be if one looked away and then back all of a sudden. Again and again I asked myself if what I was seeing was *real* — again and again the answer was *yes* although admittedly it was real in another dimension.

I wafted in and out of feelings of motion sickness. It didn't feel like a chemical reaction inside my stomach. Instead, the sickness came from having no horizon. Like a boat passenger who gets seasick below deck in rough seas, I began to feel queasy. I tried to find a horizon but there was none. There is no *up and down* in hyperspace, no right and left or north and south.

I realized I was in for a long and difficult night, and that this was going to be *work*.

Sitting or lying down made little difference to how I felt, although I found that lying down flat with my arms to my side settled my stomach. I spent most of the evening in this position. My notes say,

> This is also the position where the visions are most intense. If I want to soften the visions, I can sit up, but then the motion sickness returns.

Mother Ayahuasca is a wonderful teacher, but she exacts a price for her lessons, and that is physical discomfort. (In later ayahuasca ceremonies back home, the feeling of seasickness disappeared.) I wasn't able to fall asleep, though I eventually felt tired. I had to just stay with it.

I'm here now, I kept saying to myself. *I might as well tough it out and learn what the medicine has to teach me. I have the rest of my life to get a good night's sleep.*

Amaringo stood up at one point and sprayed some sort of liquid from inside his mouth (*aqua de flora* perhaps) three times over our heads. He appeared to be clearing the space, purifying it somehow.

I learned over the hours that followed that my thoughts had a huge impact on how I felt. If I focused on the feeling of needing to vomit, that feeling grew. If I concentrated instead on the visions and patterns, I forgot about feeling sick, at times completely. I was thankful for that!

In between icaros, perhaps two hours into the evening, I allowed myself a break from the visions and turned my thoughts to feelings of gratitude. I realized I wasn't going to experience diarrhea as some others seemed to be suffering, judging from their frequent trips to the bathrooms. I checked myself periodically and realized I couldn't use the bathroom even if I wanted to! I heard others puking loudly near me and on the other side of the room.

Buckets filled with slurpy, gurgling sounds. I started to wish I could throw up as this would lessen my nausea. But this never happened.

I lay in the darkness thinking how fortunate I was, that my preparation appeared to be paying off. I'd maintained a plain ayahuasca diet for some time. Not perfect, but enough, it appeared. I'd eaten healthily for a long time anyway, mostly raw vegetarian with lots of green smoothies and homemade granola and salads. This appeared to please the plant spirit, as well as my sexual abstinence for God knows how many months, and my deliberate effort to be a good father to my two sons, putting on an excellent Christmas for them before coming to Peru, and spending all of Christmas Day (after they went to their mother's) cleaning my apartment, tidying up and putting an extra spit polish on everything.

My house and my life were in order. I'd come prepared!

I also had a feeling — which grew in intensity in the next ceremony — that I was being given credit for my almost 25 years of work as an environmental journalist. Like a university that accepts credits from other institutions, ayahuasca appeared to recognize I'd worked to protect the environment for many years. Although this wasn't clear to me on the first night, I was about to be shown amazing things. I was 53 years old when I attended this ceremony, and ayahuasca had plans for me. She seemed to realize I don't have as much time as the twenty-somethings who were beside me, writhing and retching.

How strange all this must sound to anyone who has never interacted with a teacher plant!

In the first ceremony I was shown the Google home page of the ayahuasca realm: there was an organic software feeling to what I was seeing. I was reminded of the scrolling green numbers in *The Matrix* film trilogy. Another analogy is the lead character Jake Sully in James Cameron's epic film *Avatar*, who uses virtual reality technology to enter the world of the Na'vi on the planet Pandora, discovering a spirit-imbued forest under threat from the mining operations of human beings.

I was beyond the consensus paradigm for much of the evening, as my detailed notes from the next morning reflect:

> The medicine conveys to me somehow that I will not see beings, entities or elf-like creatures this evening. Aya wants to show me that other visual elements and textures are possible, and so various indescribable phantasmagoric scenes are presented, like surrealist paintings by Max Ernst in which cathedrals and vast landscapes are teased from dripping paint and random splashes of turpentine. Yet unlike such static pictures, these images are moving and dynamic.

Elsewhere I noted,

> It's like being inside a video game, but vastly more complex.

The ceremony lasted about four hours before it started to wind down, around the same time as the noise picked up from the nearby town celebrating the New Year. Distant music pulsed and I heard fireworks.

It's 2014! I realized.

The shamans took a break from their icaros and talked casually among themselves, occasionally laughing. The evening became relaxed all of a sudden.

I lay on my mat feeling gratitude. What a privilege, being accepted into this sacred and ancient space. I had partaken in the sacrament of an indigenous people, who shared it freely with me, allowing me inside the holy of holies of their culture. I had survived. I had not lost my mind. I had taken the teacher plant inside my body, and surrendered to her instruction.

I briefly stepped outside the maloka and looked up into the night sky. The familiar spine of the Milky Way loomed above the dark canopy of trees, like the iridescent ceiling of a Persian mosque.

My feeling for these people was as far away as is possible from the colonist's impression of *primitive tribes*. Or any stereotype. I recognized, from the inside, that they're the custodians of a many-thousands-years-old profoundly human culture whose cathedrals and spires exist in a landscape just outside the perceptual boundaries of ordinary experience.

A feeling of sorrow rose up as I thought about the wanton destruction and genocide inflicted on these people — all the Amazon people — by invaders and colonists, the turn-of-the-century rubber barons and modern pastoralists with their chainsaws and grazing cattle.

The penalty in the upper Amazon for a slave rubber worker caught trying to escape was to have the soles of their feet cut off...

I was glad I'd declined an offer in the middle of the ceremony of a second cup of ayahuasca brew. This was enough to absorb in my first ayahuasca ceremony. I suffered no violent purging, no nightmares, nothing to fear or regret.

As I returned to my mat, I was thankful for the icaros that started up again briefly. The songs of Ersilia, the female shaman, moved me to tears. I had never heard such beautiful, mournful singing. I've read that the indigenous people of the Amazon have a tragic view of life, and her songs spoke to this, to bittersweet loss and the passing of time.

Then I started to hear something new.

Very high up and far away, an angelic choir — made up of hundreds of voices — female voices — was singing in chorus with Ersilia.
I couldn't tell if she was copying their melody or if they were accom-
panying hers. I was astonished and more than a little unsettled by
this development, which mirrored the concept of angelic choirs in
Christian folklore.

Could they be one and the same?

I navigated in what I started to think of as the Akashic Field, the
woven pattern of the universe's memories. My feelings became gentler
and my nausea lifted completely. My mind floated like a boat bump-
ing gently against a dock, buoyed by an ocean of consciousness, the
cosmic background that was here before I was born and to which I'll
return when I die.

There's no sense of time here, I thought.

Except time did return. Amaringo spoke some words in Spanish,
which Rapha translated loosely as, "The ceremony is now closed." We
were invited to stay a while or return to our rooms.

I lay on the mat for a long time, suspended like an embryo in the
womb, my only distraction being flashes of light from people lighting
up hand-rolled *mapachos* made from strong tobacco — considered a
sacred plant. The smell is sweeter than that of North American commercial cigarettes as there are no additives, but nevertheless it caused
my nausea to return. I toyed for a while with the idea that there should
be *No Smoking* malokas.

I thought about the violent downpour from the storm that passed
most of the night, about which I was only faintly aware, lost in my
reverie. Much of the night became a blur. I recall receiving a song
from Erjomenes at one point, and being guided to him by Anna with
her subdued flashlight. I recall kicking over the plastic bucket at the
end of my mat, but being unconcerned as it only contained an inch
or so of water.

Erjomenes had performed a ritual of touching my forehead, my
temples and the crown of my head, concluding with strong upward
movements and blowing. I felt he had somehow detected something
that I'd withheld from the shamans, which was that I'd been using
hemp oil to fight a precancerous growth on my forehead, the second

such growth I'd detected within two years. The doctor back home had told me not to be concerned, that it was nonmalignant, but he'd burned off the first one with liquid nitrogen on the end of a Q-tip. I had a very small scar from that. I had somewhat tested the shamans by not disclosing this medical concern. And here was Erjomenes working on exactly that area.

As the energy in the maloka faded I began to feel it was safe to return to my *tambo*.

I gathered up my belongings and strode out into the night air, making my way into the room and organizing my bed, being careful to tuck in my mosquito netting on all sides of the mattress. It felt wonderful to lie down and drift into sleep, though this did not come quickly. The laser light show continued inside my head (and perhaps outside of it) for some time. I noticed the geometric patterns increasing when I focused on certain thoughts and questions, and fading when my mind was less active.

At some point Jun Jun entered the room to check on things, then left. I assumed he went back to socialize in the maloka, but I soon fell into my own realm of dreams, tossing and turning. It wasn't a deep sleep but whatever sleep it was, it was welcome.

Human beings are not born once and for all on the day their mothers give birth to them, but ... life obliges them over and over again to give birth to themselves.

— GABRIEL GARCÍA MÁRQUEZ

You must not survive a meeting with the guru.

— MOOJI, May 26, 2015

We had the next day off after our first ceremony, and everyone found different ways to relax around the retreat center property.

I found it enough to just walk short distances and then sit in contemplation. In addition to keeping some of the jungle creatures at bay, the imported sand covering the grounds provided the place with a Zen garden feeling.

I reflected on the previous night's visions.

Were they real?

And if so, in what sense?

One of my chief questions before ceremony had been that question. There was no easy answer. Certainly everything was *real* in terms of my mind or consciousness. No, I couldn't break a piece of it off. It felt real, however, in another sense, and one beyond the realm we call *imagination*. Having been a visual artist who, in my twenties, delved into Surrealism and connecting with my own subconscious, I was well acquainted with that landscape and its archetypes.

What I'd experienced in the tryptamine space went so far — *so very far* — beyond anything my mind had ever conceived, even after long painting sessions involving alcohol and sleep deprivation.

I ate breakfast in the common room and was joined by a few of the others from our group, the first of whom was Michael Sanders (who would go on to write a book about our trip). We exchanged summaries of our previous night's experiences. I felt hesitant to talk about it too much, fearing at that time that I'd dissipate the magic of the teachings. Wasn't this a highly personal quest, after all?

Mike disgorged a tremendous amount of material, including interactions with hooded energy beings, travel to other dimensions, and all kinds of crazy stuff. He said at one point he'd hung out inside a star. He spoke for about 15 minutes and then admitted this covered only the first half hour or so of the ceremony!

Man, he popped big! I thought.

In time I made my way to the art maloka near the back of the property where I joined Mike, who was by then busy writing down every detail of his ceremony. After sketching for a while, I did the same. Because I'd brought no electronic equipment on my trip, I made do with writing in pencil on small sheets of paper, for transcription at a later date onto my laptop computer.

Mike and I had gone straight into the most intense visionary states. I learned in later ceremonies that visions in themselves are not the only, or even the most desirable, phenomena of the medicine, but I was grateful, extremely, for this gift.

That afternoon I met briefly with Ersilia. Through an interpreter, I commented on her singing and asked about the angelic choir.

Did you also hear it? I asked. *And if so, were you copying their songs or were they following you?*

Ersilia gave me a puzzled look, like I'd just asked the dumbest question.

Of course I heard them! she answered in Spanish. *Where do you think I get the songs from?*

I was struck by the matter-of-factness of her comment concerning an event that was, for me, as strange as seeing a ghost.

After speaking with Ersilia I enjoyed interacting with the parrots and other jungle creatures, including some interesting insects and spiders. I chuckled at the baby spider monkey attached to the boot of one of the workers.

That evening I sat in the common room of a building designed for just hanging out. A couple of the guys played Monopoly and listened to Sid's story about managing his business back home, in response to which each of us offered advice. Rapha held small private conferences with each of us to review the events of the night before.

Eventually I made my way back to my *tambo* and fell asleep. The following day I arose and engaged in much the same low-energy activity, waiting for our next ceremony with a combination of excitement and trepidation.

CEREMONY TWO

Our next ayahuasca experience was scheduled for the night of January 2, 2014. Once again we skipped dinner, and each had a floral shower.

This time, at 6:00 pm, we enjoyed a short yoga session with Rapha in the main maloka. He was an excellent teacher and it felt good to relax into my body before ceremony. I changed again into my ceremonial white cotton clothing with the bright Shipibo designs.

As before, the curanderos entered the maloka at 8:00 pm and the second ceremony started shortly thereafter.

For this evening I had set my intention as *healing whatever inside me may prevent deeper relationships*. I wanted the medicine to open me up to all possibilities, and make sure nothing inside would prevent real intimacy.

This intention had been communicated by the assistants Rapha and Anna to the senior curanderos during a short debriefing we'd had that morning (*conversación*). At this meeting Maestro Amaringo was more on top of things, having recovered from the drowsiness of the plant dieta he'd recently concluded.

Amaringo had listened to a short recap of each of our experiences the night before, with translation provided by Rapha. I noticed Amaringo made no big to-do about people's wild journeys or visions. This was all familiar territory to him, and he was most concerned that people learn from their own journey and that the shamans be well prepared to guide us with their songs in the next ceremony.

Amaringo instructed our group to *concentrate, concentrate, concentrate* on our intentions, to work hard, and not just be distracted by simple colors and patterns. He made a passing comment also, that *only what we contribute to the community really counts in the game of life; what we do only for ourselves is of little value.*

Amaringo extolled us to sit up as much as possible during ceremony and not lie flat on our mats, which exacerbates the experience of being overwhelmed.

That had been in the morning, and here I was again drinking the pungent tea and returning to my mat. I lay in the dark for about 40 minutes anticipating ayahuasca's effects. Again my heart raced in anticipation. And again the texture of the sticky liquid made me feel like throwing up, more than the taste. That sensation passed quickly.

As before, geometric patterns appeared — outlines in color — first a deep red and then green and other colors of laser-like intensity. However, I made a deliberate effort not to pay too much attention to the patterns and focused, as Amaringo had suggested, on my intention.

This led to a full-blown experience that had nothing to do with the patterns.

While I was sitting upright with legs crossed, the entire maloka seemed to sway back and forth, like a gigantic pendulum. I looked around in the dark to see if anyone else was feeling this. The movement was dramatic and I clutched my mat, trying to hold on. Yet I appeared to be the only person sensing this motion.

I wondered what was happening — and then realized I was inside my mother's womb. The rocking back and forth was the swaying of her hips as she walked.

A profound and healing emotion rose from inside me as I reconnected with this deep memory and was reminded of the connection between mother and child — my mother and me. I also felt a telepathic sense of being loved by a universal mother — Gaia herself — cradling me in her body in the dark, walking.

Later I realized that this experience related to my interest in having blocks against loving relationships removed. I was overwhelmed by the sense of connection.

> Unis unites with the mother and becomes the child within her, as the Tantric initiate unites with the mother in order to be reborn. As in Tantra, the holy vision is opened to the initiate by means of the rising of the heightened electricity within the body, the internal serpent, prompted by real or imagined union. The rising of this energy prompts the birth of the eye, omniscience, the child or successful fruit of the practice. Thus it is only when the initiate merges with the mother that he sees the holy aspects revealed.
>
> — SUSAN BRIND MORROW,
> *The Dawning of the Moon of the Mind:*
> *Unlocking the Pyramid Texts*

The next experience was one that also started with me sitting up straight with legs crossed. I used pillows to support my back.

I felt a strong energy in the center of my body (the heart chakra) and was invited to look down, which I did slowly, and to place my hand on my heart. I felt this message was being conveyed by Amaringo and perhaps the other curanderos telepathically, though in that space it could have been directly from the ayahuasca itself.

Amazingly, I was able to see my heart! But it was not the red heart of my physical body. Rather, it was a golden heart — a heart of the spirit realm. It beat steadily and was radiant. It looked like it was made of burnished gold. Light poured from it and I could direct energy from my right hand into the spirit heart.

I remembered my Reiki training from a few months before, and realized I was being shown how to heal my own heart, and maintain it, with Reiki energy. I was moving, seeing and feeling this spiritual heart, coming to know its existence for the first time.

I was told — not in words but through a kind of feeling — that I must embrace my *warrior heart* and that women admire men who invest wisely in their warrior heart energy. (The idea of the warrior was not violent, but more in the way of standing up for what one knows is right.)

Then I lay down as though being directed to do so telepathically. Somehow the idea was conveyed to me that I was to undergo an operation. I then had a keen sense of being operated on by the curanderos, who focused on my spirit heart like a surgical team. A song specifically directed to me (it seemed) accompanied this.

I felt myself slipping into unconsciousness and was told repeatedly to stay awake, that there was great peril in falling asleep during this procedure! I was told to keep breathing, which I did. I found it difficult work to breathe and remain awake. But I persisted. I was warned there was a real risk of injury or death if I slept at this time!

Next it was transmitted silently that I should sit up and pay attention. At this point Amaringo coughed up enormous amounts of phlegm and bile into his plastic bucket. It was extraordinary how much he evicted from his throat. This went on for a long time with dramatic sounds. I remember reading in Stephan Beyer's book *Singing to the Plants* how Amazonian shamans make a big show of displaying how they can suck the illness from a person and throw it up; the description there made it sound like a con job to impress a gullible audience. But here in that maloka I felt there was simply no way a human being could spit up so much bile, for so long, or fake what I was witnessing and hearing.

I was told (again telepathically) to observe, with words something like, *He's doing this for you! The least you can do is pay attention!*

It was clear the bile and phlegm had been removed from around my heart. While it could have included sickness from others in the room, I had a strong sense that most of it was mine, and I silently thanked Amaringo for doing this for me. I wondered at the strength of shamans, and their willingness to do this difficult work for their clients.

With my golden spirit heart cleared of this blockage a vital energy flowed through me and I became very open. The bushmen of the Kalahari call this the heart becoming *softened.* Perhaps it was this openness that set the stage for what transpired next, which was unpleasant. I was definitely coming off the first big peak from the first cup of ayahuasca, but I was still in its thrall.

How to describe what happened next! Perhaps it's to say that *I had my ass handed to me* by the ayahuasca spirit. I endured a tough lesson in humility.

For about an hour I felt tremendous shame as the medicine revealed to me my own narcissism in coming to Peru to experience ayahuasca. It was as though the plant was saying, *So, asshole, you thought you'd come down here and drink this brew and then go home and brag to your friends about it, huh?* or *So you thought you'd become the 'cool guy' back home with all your New Age friends, having done the 'real deal' aya ceremony? Huh, asshole?*

It was more of a feeling than a message with words, although sometimes words and thoughts were included.

It went on like that for a long time, and like a puppy having its nose rubbed in the spot where it peed on the carpet, I was made to look at the curanderos singing their icaros while being reminded they had invited me into their sacred space and shared their ancient secrets, and here I was, the rich gringo wearing their "folkloric costume" like a total fraud, ripping off their culture to feed my ego and get some kind of healing for self-centered purposes.

It went beyond even that, as the nature of the colonial settler culture was revealed to me, of which I'm a manifestation. I later thought of it as being cured of a disease of European culture that the First Nations people call *wetiko.*

My head hung in shame as I felt like the New Age version of a rubber baron, feeling suddenly ridiculous in the Shipibo pants and tunic I was wearing.

Look at the shape of this room, asshole, the medicine said, as I noticed it was round — round as in inclusive, a container where all are equal.

This is about community, the medicine told me, *not just about you.*

Eventually I couldn't take it any more and, gathering my flashlight and water bottle, I stood up on shaky legs and made my way through the darkness across the wide maloka floor and out the door into the evening air. A night assistant's flashlight guided me from afar as I made my way back to my room, where I took off the ceremonial clothing and changed into my regular T-shirt and shorts.

I stood there, not sure what to do. Part of me wanted to just go to bed and sleep. Hadn't the medicine worn off anyway? But I felt bad about walking out on the ceremony. I should be there for my friends, I thought, to show support for them, and appreciation for the shamans who were working so hard for all our benefit.

I had just decided to return when Anna appeared at my door and asked me to come back with her.

You must return for your song, she said. *You'll feel a lot better.*

I agreed and said I'd come with her, except I needed to make a stop at the bathroom on the way.

When I returned to the maloka, I felt warmth and love. Ayahuasca had scolded me like a mother or grandmother teaching a lesson to a child she nevertheless loves. As long as I was genuinely humble, I was welcome in this sacred space.

I sat in front of Erjomenes and received my song. My head hung low. Shame is not the right word for what I felt. Instead, I felt humility. Real humility.

As I returned to my mat I thought the medicine had fallen off. I settled in to being present for my friends and to showing respect for the curanderos.

I was mistaken: what had transpired was only the first stage of a long and powerful evening, with much work remaining.

Ayahuasca had prepared me for a very privileged experience: she was going to show me something special, but first needed to know I was humble — *truly humble* — so I would never misuse the teaching.

I lay back on my mattress and the geometric patterns returned, very powerfully, with more brilliant light and colored edges than before. I was invited again and again to think about what I was looking at. The designs started to pulse and grow increasingly complex and three-dimensional.

What are you looking at? I was asked. *WHAT are you LOOKING AT?* it asked louder and louder.

And then I had the breakthrough. The realization fell on me hard, with the same emotion as watching the birth of a child. What I had thought before — that the geometric patterns were just a *preview* of the spirit world, or some kind of entry-level navigational tool for this realm's strange internet — was more than that. Much more.

It was — or it had now become — the very center of the organism. I was standing, or lying, in the Central Operating Unit of the mainframe computer of the universe, the brain or mind of creation.

Oh my God! I said silently and aloud. *Oh my God!* over and over again.

I was experiencing the Creator, unmediated. Though it was genderless, it felt very female and maternal. She was showing herself in the only way my limited human mind could comprehend, and I began to sob as the realization of what I was seeing sank in.

Once I *got it* and the universal consciousness knew I understood what I was seeing, she began to show herself to me in more and more complex ways.

The geometric designs modulated into more organic shapes, becoming beings, animals, insects, fish, birds... It was like an organic factory manufacturing all of life and creation, and the raw material was pure consciousness. It was as if the consciousness was saying, *This is how I make birds! This is how I make snakes! This is how I make people!*

The images were very detailed, but the finishes were otherworldly. They were made up of lines, very much like the curved lines animators use in creating 3D computer-animated creatures and objects, before they put on the digital "skin." White lines on a dark background, blueprint-style.

The creatures never fully formed or walked away. Instead, they emerged and pulsed back into the overall consciousness or organism from which they emanated. *Was this the morphogenicity that Rupert Sheldrake writes about?* I wondered. *The fields of the cosmos from which everything emerges and to which everything returns?*

I was shown how life is made, living archetypes, not the end result, with which I was already familiar.

This continued for a long time and I was overwhelmed. I kept thinking and feeling that this was a privileged sight, and I wondered why I was being shown, why I was worthy.

Later, I'd think about this a great deal, and conclude that perhaps it's because I'm a writer and communicator, and the Creator's creations are in jeopardy from human greed and avarice. For now it was all I could do to absorb and think to myself, *I must not forget this! I must remember! I must remember!*

As I came down from this peak I wondered why I had been shown no serpents, at least not in some powerful and three-dimensional way. I had read about people on ayahuasca interacting with enormous 500-meter long snakes with fluorescent skins and glowing eyes, and part of me longed to see them.

And then ayahuasca again asked me to answer my own question. Ayahuasca shows but does not tell. You must decipher her lessons for yourself, and always ask, *What is the lesson here? What is the lesson?*

It hit me hard when the answer emerged.

Why would I not see serpents? I asked myself. *How about... it's because... I am a serpent...*

I'm a serpent? I asked. *A snake?* almost out loud.

Then I realized the colors I was seeing were from some kind of light spectrum that snakes see and humans do not. I had been looking all this time through the eyes of a snake.

And then another rhetorical question emerged.

And what kind of snake doesn't see other snakes? an inner voice asked.

I pondered this for a while.

A snake of which other snakes are afraid! I said.

And then I realized I was looking through the eyes of an anaconda. And at that moment I was given this spirit animal.

Images of anacondas presented themselves in front of me, but not anacondas as they exist in this dimension. Just as my spirit heart had been gold and shining, the anaconda was golden and emitted light, and its eyes sparkled as though made from jewels. I was both looking outward through the eyes of the spirit anaconda, and into the anaconda's dazzling eyes.

How odd this must sound to anyone who has never drunk ayahuasca or another powerful entheogen. I could hardly believe it myself, yet it was an *experience*, and a *knowing*, of a sort I was later to learn is familiar to shamans, who can never adequately explain the spirit realm to people who have never entered. And it was a *knowing of the heart* — not just of the mind.

Gradually the medicine wore off and the curanderos closed the ceremony. I lay for a long time curled on my mat, listening to the shamans talk and smelling smoke from the *mapacho* cigarettes people lit up around me. I became aware of my fellow travellers in the room, who I could tell also had experienced long and difficult nights.

We had been told to sit up and pay attention; most of us had been given tough lessons, it would emerge.

I think midlife is when the universe gently places her hands upon your shoulders, pulls you close, and whispers in your ear: "I'm not screwing around. It's time. All of this pretending and performing – these coping mechanisms that you've developed to protect yourself from feeling inadequate and getting hurt – has to go.

"Your armor is preventing you from growing into your gifts. I understand that you needed these protections when you were small. I understand that you believed your armor could help you secure all of the things you needed to feel worthy of love and belonging, but you're still searching and you're more lost than ever.

"Time is growing short. There are unexplored adventures ahead of you. You can't live the rest of your life worried about what other people think. You were born worthy of love and belonging. Courage and daring are coursing through you. You were made to live and love with your whole heart. It's time to show up and be seen."

— BRENÉ BROWN

I awoke to the sound of birds at the Nihue Rao Spiritual Center on the morning of January 3, 2014.

As I lay in bed underneath mosquito netting, I pondered the challenge ahead: That I would face another ayahuasca ceremony right on the heels of the ceremony the night before, with no recovery day in between.

It never occurred to me to opt out.

Many of us spent the day resting as much as possible, but I found it difficult to sleep; my mind was buzzing from all I'd seen the night before.

My morning began with a long discussion with fellow "ayahuasca test pilot" Mike. We came across one another in the kitchen, both intent on writing down our experiences. We'd spent much of the day after our first ayahuasca journey writing in the art maloka. It was clear we were the writers of the group.

I asked Mike about his experiences the night before and this unleashed a long story of multiple lessons and travels Mike had experienced in the other dimension, and his encounters with beings. I really enjoyed Mike's stories and the confirmation from another bright and skeptical person who'd deeply entered the hyperspace realm.

We were joined by a couple of others who arrived early for breakfast. I shared highlights of my experiences from the night before. I recall being close to tears with my voice trembling. It was clear that both Mike and I were still condensing from powerful experiences. While I don't regret sharing what I'd seen, or perhaps sounding a bit odd, I reckon we must have looked like real newbies to the very experienced American woman Sita who joined us. She had sat with the shamans the night before and leads ceremonies of her own back home.

Sita — who lives in California and was involved somehow with the retreat center — made some constructive comments that helped me interpret the shamanic realms.

I looked forward to our group conversation with Amaringo in the maloka, but he didn't show up at the appointed time. It later emerged he was delayed with business in nearby Iquitos.

We had a meeting in the maloka with Rapha and Anna instead, where everyone shared their experiences. Then, later in the afternoon,

Amaringo showed up and a second meeting was called just as I was taking my flower shower in the back of the property. Each person took turns recounting their experiences while Rapha translated and Amaringo nodded knowingly, occasionally offering commentary. This curandero took interest in our experiences and offered useful advice here and there, but it was minimal. The conversation was not an opportunity to psychoanalyze us or interpret our dreams: unless there was something really wrong, he spoke little. I wondered what these curanderos thought about tourists like us from rich countries, plagued by many neuroses and "First World problems."

According to the reports, most of us had had a tough night and had worked hard through various challenges. For some the experience had been almost entirely physical and related to some sort of deep cleansing, while for others it was more mental, with lots of visuals, encounters with beings or (in my case) engaging with a massive and throbbing universal consciousness.

Prep for the third ceremony began as before with a flower shower around 4:00 pm and (of course) no dinner. Rapha informed us there would be no yoga that evening.

I felt trepidation as I relaxed in the hammock in my room, sometimes talking with roommate John, who offered pieces of sage advice that I incorporated into my intention setting and interpretation of prior events. My intention for the evening was simple: I would ask ayahuasca for guidance in integrating into my life what she had shown me the night before, and using that knowledge to create community back home, or whatever purpose she might have for me.

Some of the group would fly home the following evening. Myself, I'd added a couple of days to the trip to hang out in Iquitos and recover from what I (rightly) assumed would be a demanding experience.

CEREMONY THREE

Ceremony began as usual at 8:00 pm. I was one of the last to drink, although I noticed we were joined by a couple of new people, including Hillary — a young American woman from Los Angeles who had lived for six months in Iquitos working for a non-governmental organization affiliated with another ayahuasca center — the Temple of the Way of Light — where Rapha had also previously worked.

I lay back and waited for the medicine to hit, which it did right on cue after about 40 minutes.

Amaringo had mentioned that this evening we'd drink from a batch of ayahuasca brew that had just been freshly cooked. He told us that on the previous evenings we'd used up the vestiges of an older concoction, and that this night we should expect *strong medicine*.

This was the first time I became aware that the brew we call *ayahuasca* has varietals much like wine, and can be compared by connoisseurs much as aficionados of red wines compare grapes from different regions or different pressings, and good harvest years. The age and color of the vine, the time spent brewing, the DMT adjunct plant — even the intention and prayers held over the stripping of leaves and the cooking — may all influence the character and potency of the psychotropic concoction.

Fellow traveller Tatyana had suggested I might want to ask for a little less this time, yet for some reason when my turn came to drink I asked the assistant to pour me a little extra. I suppose that, knowing this was my last ceremony, I wanted a powerful experience, and didn't want to ask for more later.

I wasn't disappointed: the medicine was indeed powerful and the appearance of the geometric patterns initiated what may have been a six-hour journey (or possibly longer — I lost all sense of time).

While rain pounded on the roof of the maloka, as in the previous nights the experience began with the now-familiar geometric patterns, starting with red outlines, then red and green, then other colors. Again the icaros increased the effects and guided the meditation, which grew or subsided with the songs.

My field notes remind me that,

> ...overall it was a very long ceremony and night that ran the gamut of light and dark visions or experiences.

Physically I felt very weak through most of the night, with extended periods of nausea (but no vomiting or diarrhea). I remember wishing I could throw up (the very thing I'd dreaded before the first ceremony) for the relief it would bring. The only purging I had came from deep yawns and some tears.

When the medicine took hold I went through a period of regretting the whole thing, wishing I could avoid what I knew was in store. There was no comfortable position, no way of escaping the seasickness. I felt dizzy when I sat up. When I lay down, the nausea subsided, but then I felt dark forces engulfing me, as though lying down brought me closer to the grave. Shadowy insects and parasites would devour me, so I'd sit up again. I spent much of the night propped up in a compromise position, leaning back on pillows, staring at the ceiling.

However, much as I suffered, I was keen for the visions and teachings, and kept reminding myself it would all be worth it. I focused on my intention, which was surprisingly difficult.

Integration... I would manage here and there. Or... *Community, I must focus on community...*

God but this was demanding work!

There were too many visions and teachings to ever recount, but it's fair to say that the third ceremony built on the previous two, like the third act in a play. Overall the visions were more vivid and more three-dimensional.

I'm thankful for the detailed notes I made the following morning, while everything was fresh, because dark events late in the experience made it otherwise difficult to recall the positive lessons I received early in the night.

The first lesson was loving and gentle. I felt relief that ayahuasca was showing me her nurturing side.

Perhaps this would be a gentle night after all.

I was shown how the answer to my questions around integration lay within the question itself. I had grown up surrounded with quite a bit of anger and dysfunction, with divorced parents and no small amount of alcohol abuse on one side, and a strained relationship with my stepfather on the other. This had trained me to initially *react* to situations, often with anger as the conditioned response. I needed to reprogram my initial reaction to events and challenges, softening it and acting from a position of humility and compassion.

My heart flooded again with the feeling of humility from the previous night's lessons. I was taught to start each and every time from this position of humility, which would then translate into actions of love and kindness.

Remember to look through the eyes of the sacred anaconda, whenever challenges arise, I was told.

Next I was invited to always remember the *ayahuasca dimension of reality* that operates in the background of our normal dimension, like the programming in *The Matrix*. The forces at work in that other dimension interact with and affect this one. We might, for instance, feel anger or jealousy or some other emotion, thinking it's because of the actions of another person, when it may actually be a dark energy permeating from the other side. Clearing up dark energy and letting the light in is an ongoing process, I learned. (Where this information came from, I can't honestly say.)

I'd normally be skeptical of this kind of energy work, but it all made sense in this realm of pure consciousness.

The next lesson was profound.

I was told to be careful about how I *intervene* in various situations. I learned that sometimes intervention deprives other beings of their *teaching moments*. Whether they learn from them or not, it's their karma in this life's journey to have experiences and learn from them; I am not responsible for their experiences. In a difficult situation in which someone's actions or reactions pose a threat to others, it's reasonable for each of us to redirect a person or, if that fails, protect the weak and innocent.

But I must not interrupt someone else's teaching moments, I learned.

I was shown various situations from my own life where I could have changed things up instead of reacting in a predictable way. These were situations where I could have embraced my warrior heart and acted from humility and compassion instead of reacting and lashing out.

Remember the sparkling eyes of the anaconda and her teachings, I heard. Healing and the creation of community would follow.

As the icaros trailed off I struggled again with nausea and discomfort. I wondered at the fact that this teacher plant was living up to that title. I wondered also whether there would be more lessons.

As the next song began I was hit with a big download that expanded on the last teaching. To some extent, the previous lesson could have been delivered by Dr. Phil, but the next one showcased the plant spirit's awesome power. Over what felt like a very long time, I was shown what I call the *Story of the Mother*.

In essence, the mother's is the most universal and constant story. The universal mother — cosmic consciousness — creates all reality. I was shown how — at the macro level — she creates galaxies that are in turn the mother to stars, that are in turn the mother to planets, that are in turn the mother to ecosystems, that are in turn the mother to plants, animals, insects, birds and fish, and microscopic organisms. At every level the experience of the mother is both beautiful and sad; although mothers experience the joy of creation, giving birth, they pay a price — always — which is the pain of setting their offspring free, of saying goodbye.

Mothers must come to terms with the fact that after all the kindness and nurturing they show the beings they create, their children will leave to pursue their own lives. The mother must not interfere, even though it breaks her heart to see them go, for otherwise she prevents her offspring from fulfilling their own destinies.

Recounted this way, the lesson sounds powerful enough. But ayahuasca made me *feel* the mother's pain, to *feel* her suffering as she says goodbye, and it was *beyond what I could endure*. I felt the pain of many mothers, like the female leopard that nudges its cubs out into the world and turns her back on them, forcing them off into their own adventures. I was shown human mothers saying goodbye, hiding their pain. I embodied a cascade of all mothers' pain from the greatest cosmic level down to the microscopic. I remember feeling the universe creating galaxies and then letting go of them. I remember feeling the spider laying her eggs in the safest place, suspending them on silk threads, knowing she won't be alive when they hatch.

Somewhere in the midst of this I was again informed of my role as a male, as a *warrior*.

Again, the warrior was not a violent image, but related to the warrior's duty to protect mothers and their offspring. I was shown ways in which I could improve my honoring and helping my own mother, and also my ex-wife, mother to my children.

Then the lesson expanded and built at a cosmic level on the earlier lesson about not interfering with people's *teaching moments*. A lesson manifested about accepting, like a mother, the destiny of other people, other creatures, and in fact *whole civilizations and ecosystems*. Much as I'm disturbed by the appalling harm humans are inflicting on the natural environment, and how this could trigger an eventual collapse of civilization, I was shown how this is nevertheless part of an ageless cycle of life, death and rebirth. The body of one life, society or ecosystem becomes the compost from which the next manifestation arises. I saw how many earlier eras and life forms (from the Cambrian period, the Age of the Dinosaurs, the Age of the Megafauna, etc.) passed, which was sad for them, but allowed for human beings to arise (for example).

We too will eventually pass from this world, taking down ecosystems with us, but who can say what will take our place, and that it will necessarily be worse? The Creator will continue minting new life forms from her infinite creativity. The process will go on and on, everywhere in the universe. We are not so special after all.

It's not that God *wants* human beings to destroy themselves, or harm the environment. Again, this is the point of the Story of the Mother. She created us and now must let us go. Why create us at all if she's going to micromanage us?

Yet she is not uncaring. She cares for us more deeply than we know, and feels a mother's pain when we make mistakes or inflict harm on ourselves and her other creations. She listens to us when we approach her through ayahuasca and other sacred plants, and she shows us the truth if we ask for it. But she never commands what to do: we must solve the riddles ourselves and make our own decisions.

I was also shown that each and every creature has an equally valid life, from the perspective of Mother Earth. Each of those tiny cutter ants we'd seen a few days before on the jungle floor, transporting their leaf treasures to their enormous ant hill, were as important and valid as any other being in her eyes. We delude ourselves thinking that some famous person living in New York, getting the best seats in restaurants, and appearing on TV is more important in the grand scheme of things than ants or snakes or fish that live their entire lives unknown to human beings.

And they don't need our help, at least not exactly. We need to respect their work: spiders have a job to do, as do flies. We need to appreciate them and stay out of their way. The spider doesn't fret about the experience of the fly; the fly doesn't ponder the perspective of the spider: each has a life to live and its own teaching moments.

It sounds flat, recounting the teaching like this, but I was made to *feel* many of these lessons from the perspective of the animals and insects themselves. It was experiential and not some kind of college lecture. There were generally no words at all.

After this lesson I went through a blurry stage of sickness, as though a price was being exacted from my body in exchange for the teachings. I thought about the strength and courage of curanderos. How, I asked, can they endure this night after night, week after week, year after year? I thought of them as Olympic athletes, achieving extraordinary feats in the dark surroundings of malokas and jungle lodges, more or less unrecognized by the outside world.

This was only my third ceremony and I felt beat! Utterly whipped!

I struggled to hold on as the first lessons ended and the visions dropped off. I sat through my song with Erjomenes, and hoped that perhaps the night was winding down and I'd be able to return to my room to sleep.

But this was not to be. At all. The last stage of the night lasted for many hours and was dark, in every sense.

I was shown visions of dying and felt myself sinking into the earth, into the dirt, with the grass above me, and earthworms and insects all around. I thought if maybe I sat up I could elude these visions, but I remained in a prone position.

I wasn't sure that I could sit up anyway.

I wondered why I was being shown this or, more accurately, made to *feel* this, and then I remembered an intention I had set (without thinking of it that way) before I even came to Peru: I had wanted to see where my stepfather went after he died the previous spring. I felt that seeing the Creator — the cosmic consciousness — had already answered that question. We come from, and return to, that great pulsing intelligence that permeates everything.

But there is another side to death — actual physical death — that I was being shown, almost against my will. The medicine was saying telepathically, *So, you really want to know what death feels like, do you?* with me pleading, *No, no, I don't need to experience this!* Again and again I felt myself sinking down into my mat, prostrate on my back or lying sideways, looking up at the earth and grass above me, unable to move, unable to lift my hand or head.

Everything was over.

I experienced the death of the body, so different from the liberation of consciousness.

I believe I actually died at one point.

Was this a *shamanic death*, as I'd read about?

For a while there was no *me* to ponder these questions.

This was certainly a lesson in being careful about what one asks for. At least, that's what I thought when my body brought itself back to life, with a great rousing inhalation. I hadn't been breathing for a while. I don't know how long.

* * *

Re-awoken, I had to fight my way back to ordinary reality. With all the energy I could summon, I eventually sat up and slowly reoriented myself to the space in the maloka. I heard Amaringo say something in Spanish and assumed (wrongly) that the ceremony had concluded. The curanderos were talking, like musicians taking a break.

The contrast was stark between the curanderos casually speaking with one another and the terminal place from which I'd just returned.

I focused on the spatial coordinates of this dimension and finally navigated myself into a standing position. Flashlight and water bottle in hand, I headed out into the night air to use the bathroom. I found it easily and regained my composure.

The sky was overcast — no stars — but it had stopped raining. I entered one of the open bathroom stalls. A candle burned in the corner, on the floor.

I sat on the toilet for a long while, and then had the most extraordinary experience. Ayahuasca was going to show me lessons even as I sat on the toilet!

And it was really freaky William S. Burroughs stuff.

I looked down at the concrete bathroom floor, which was stained and discolored, like an old wall. As I did so, a powerful hallucination took hold. I gradually noticed that the floor was not made of concrete, but of thick ice, with large cracks in the center. The more I looked, the more convincing the illusion appeared. Intellectually I knew this was a completely solid concrete floor, and yet it was semitransparent ice, and if I moved my head from side to side, the perspective of the deep cracks shifted perfectly in three-dimensions.

I closed my eyes and looked again, but nothing I did could shake the illusion.

Then I noticed there were forms moving beneath the ice — shadowy vines and algae, then creatures, serpentine and mysterious. I began to worry that if I looked much longer the creatures would develop into something frightening, or might surface through the ice. Yet I couldn't tear myself away — it was just so damn interesting!

Everything else in the room looked normal: the sink and mirror, the overflowing waste basket, the candle in its dish on the floor... but the floor itself was an ice-covered river.

Fortunately, I thought to go past the mere visual aspect of what I was seeing and asked myself, *What is the lesson here?*

After thinking about it for a few minutes the answer came. And it was one of the most powerful lessons from my whole trip to Peru.

The floor was solid, I realized, but the spirit of ayahuasca — or *the universe* if you prefer — could turn it into a sheet of ice with creatures underneath if she wanted. She could create anything she liked for my mind to experience. The teaching was not simply that I was seeing a mirage, a hallucination: rather, the teaching was that my *entire world* is a hallucination... *everywhere and at all times.*

I was seeing how consensus reality is created, by having it perturbed in this undeniably realistic way. The universe, I had read in physics articles, might be holographic. It's certainly made up of fractals. Of quanta. Of information.

And here I was, seeing it.

I will always know and remember now that we are like Neo in *The Matrix*— every seemingly solid wall, floor, table — even the concrete

floor of a bathroom — is a manifestation synthesized from consciousness, or at least a negotiated reality. Our minds fix in place a realm to
live in, in this dimension, made from energy and consciousness, of the
very same material as the realm I had entered in my ayahuasca visions.
Eventually I remembered Rapha's instruction not to hang out too
long outside the maloka or in the bathrooms. The *arkana* — the magic
circle of protection, which felt very real for me — was strongest in the
container of the maloka.

I washed my hands and made my way back to the sacred space, lay
down on my mat, and assumed (wrongly again) that my evening was
largely over.

I felt exhausted — more tired at a deep body level than I can remember ever feeling.

I sank down into the mat and, after a while, became aware I'd been
lying there for a long time. The icaros continued and I became vaguely
aware that the ceremony hadn't ended. The whole time I'd been in the
bathroom the ceremony had been fully underway.

I began to see insect silhouettes around me, mostly spiders, and felt
I was again going to be taught something, although this time it would
concern my fears, as I am (or was) an arachnophobe.

It dawned on me slowly that I was paralyzed. More precisely, I'd
been venomized by an enormous spider of the black widow type,
with a large abdomen. I saw her from the perspective of a fly: she was
larger than me.

I was pinned to the mat and couldn't raise my hands or head no
matter how hard I tried. I was stuck in her web.

I kept slipping out of consciousness, only to wake up and realize
again and again I hadn't been breathing.

I had to deliberately inflate my chest and force myself to breath, in
great gasps. I felt I was in real trouble but was unable to ask for help.
In fact, I was so venomized that calling for help didn't occur to me. I
just lay there, semi-comatose, for what must have been an hour, possibly more.

I watched the spider come and go, going about her business. I was
being stored, kept alive for later consumption. This no longer felt like
a lesson from the plant medicine; instead, I felt I was under the spell

of a sinister force. I wondered if my lingering in the washroom stall outside the maloka had created an opportunity for this dark entity to slip inside. My slipping into unconsciousness for long periods and awakening gasping for air was not a hallucination: I was truly fighting for my life now, and I was losing.

Thankfully, at some point Amaringo detected this dark force, perhaps even my predicament, and jumped to his feet. He strode forcefully across the maloka, stepped toward me and blew some kind of liquid forcefully into the air above me, and the people to my left.

The dark energy retreated almost immediately, and the spiders scuttled away.

Yet I was still venomized and incoherent. I later decided that if such events ever again transpire, I'll call for help, even if doing so requires that I strain with every fiber of my being. I'm not sure that I could have.

I don't remember which happened first: the ceremony ending or my ripping myself from the grip of the spider's poison, but I eventually realized I needed to fight my way out of this situation. I recalled ayahuasca's lessons and how she could create any creature at will.

You want spiders? I can give you spiders, she had said. *You want snakes, I can give you snakes.*

I focused my attention on different animals and insects and reptiles until, after a long time, the impression of spiders faded and I slowly roused myself.

What a struggle that was!

In time I was able to sit up, but then lay back down again, weak.

I found myself listening to the conversation of Sita and Hillary to my right, who were fully alert and "in the moment" in a way I envied. They seemed so far away...

The normality of their conversation was like a rope floating on the sea of consciousness that I used to gradually pull myself back toward the raft of normality.

I have ambivalent feelings retelling the story of the spiders and my poisoning in the spirit realm. At some level I wonder if it really happened in the way I remember. But the notes I wrote down the following morning don't lie. They even recall how I continued to remind myself to breathe well into the morning, when I'd take a gulp of air. I'd been afraid to fall asleep.

I also don't wish to turn people off who are considering ayahuasca, by telling frightening stories. Yet I feel responsible to share this tale, as it underscores the importance of drinking ayahuasca in the presence of a skilled and experienced shaman. God only knows what would have happened if that dark energy had got hold of me and there was no one around to dispel it!

I'd encountered real forces of danger in a dimension about which I knew almost nothing. I don't believe I'd have lived.

Interestingly, in the group conversation the following morning, when I recalled this story Amaringo said he'd seen the spiders too, which is why he'd jumped up and dispelled them. He told us in detail how a dark energy had taken over the inner ceiling of the maloka structure a few months prior, that took the form of giant spiders, and how he and the other curanderos had fought and dispelled them finally by blowing a spicy liquid at them.

He told me this dark energy did not emerge from inside me, but was a force from outside.

As Amaringo confirmed my suspicions, I lay on my mat looking up at the wooden beams whose wagon wheel structure held the building together. They looked like great spider webs; the dubiousness of installing such a shape in a maloka was not lost on me. Maybe they have to be built that way, but a rectangular support structure would be a better choice, in my opinion. Anything but a spider's web!

This is where my notes end.

* * *

The day after the third ceremony we lingered, all of us, and daydreamed, compared notes, or lost ourselves in conversation.

It was with a sweet sadness that I said goodbye to the first bunch of travelers who departed in mototaxis. They were heading for Iquitos where we'd all share one final dinner before the group broke up and everyone faced the long journey home.

Mike, Sid and Carl were the first to go, young men in their twenties with so much in store for them: careers, marriage, children, successes and failures — all of them now transformed by their encounter with the vine of souls.

This must have been what it felt like, I thought, saying goodbye to one's platoon mates at the end of a tour of duty in Vietnam as helicopters arrived and the soldiers sat on their duffle bags, smoking one last cigarette together.

I stayed in Iquitos for two more days, first saying goodbye to my roommate Jun Jun, perhaps the most transformed of all of us, who planned to move from his apartment in Tampa, Florida to one of the more remote islands in Hawaii. He had discovered his true identity as a healer, and I wished him well. We shared one final hug before his mototaxi arrived and he headed off into his new life.

I spent most of my final time in Iquitos hanging around the Karma Kafe (a gringo magnet) where I made friends with a young man from Norway and had some long conversations with Hillary, who was at the end of her NGO contract and planned to visit friends in Brazil.

Eventually I took my final leave of the tour organizers, Dan and Tatyana, and flagged down a mototaxi. It took me more than 24 hours to fly home to Toronto, where the temperatures were minus 15 degrees Celsius and my car was buried under a foot of snow at the outdoor airport parking lot.

At the time, home for me was a small town about two hours northeast of Toronto. I wrote a journal entry after returning:

Four days have passed and I'm home in Collingwood. My sleep is deep now and my dreams are not disturbing. I don't know how long it will last, but sometimes when I close my eyes and really focus, I can see those geometric patterns in the darkness, with their red outlines, that I used to see in ayahuasca ceremonies.

They're faint, but they're there. Perhaps Mother Ayahuasca is inside me now, and will be with me forever.

I certainly hope so.

The very meaninglessness of life forces man to create his own meaning. Children, of course, begin life with an untarnished sense of wonder, a capacity to experience total joy at something as simple as the greenness of a leaf; but as they grow older, the awareness of death and decay begins to impinge on their consciousness and subtly erode their *joie de vivre*, their idealism — and their assumption of immortality. As a child matures, he sees death and pain everywhere about him, and begins to lose faith in the ultimate goodness of man. But if he's reasonably strong — and lucky — he can emerge from this twilight of the soul into a rebirth of life's *élan*. Both because of and in spite of his awareness of the meaninglessness of life, he can forge a fresh sense of purpose and affirmation. He may not recapture the same pure sense of wonder he was born with, but he can shape something far more enduring and sustaining. The most terrifying fact about the universe is not that it is hostile but that it is indifferent; but if we can come to terms with this indifference and accept the challenge of life within the boundaries of death — however mutable man may be able to make them — our existence as a species can have genuine meaning and

fulfillment. However vast the darkness, we must supply
our own light.

— STANLEY KUBRIK

Whenever dharma declines and the purpose of life is
forgotten, I manifest myself on earth. I am born in every
age to protect the good, to destroy evil, and to reestab-
lish dharma.

— LORD KRISHNA, *Bhagavad Gita*

I didn't know — couldn't have known — how my life would change
when I returned to Canada from Peru. I supposed that ayahuasca had
changed me, but in what ways?

At the retreat center I'd drunk the medicine three times, and had
"popped big" with full-blown visions, psychedelic carpet rides and
profound lessons from the teacher plant. I felt everything shift inside
me, but many changes took time to show up in the weeks and months
that followed.

At the time I lived in a two-bedroom condominium that I rented in
a gated community. Although I'm more of a city person, I lived there
in order to be closer to my teenage sons, who lived in that town with
their mother. They stayed with me from Thursday evening to Monday
evening, every other weekend.

I worked as editor of two trade magazines owned by a Canadian
media conglomerate based in Toronto, to which my partners and I
had sold the publications back in 2000. I'd been a partner-owner of
the small publishing company that produced them for the previous
decade, starting in late 1989.

I worked from home and visited the head office for meetings a couple
of times a month. I also maintained friendships in the city, knowing I'd
return when my kids were older. When I visited the city I'd usually stay
with my mother, who had been widowed the year before my Peru trip.

One thing I noticed right away when I settled back into my life was
that my tendency to occasionally self-medicate with alcohol was gone.

I'd never been a heavy drinker, but the stress of my divorce in the mid-2000's had triggered a habit of sipping rye whisky in the evenings. I've always liked English pub ales, but never so much as to abuse them. One or two pints and I'm fine. I like good red wines, but again, not so much as to overindulge.

But rye whiskey kind of snuck up on me. I developed a taste for it, especially sipping it with ice while I played guitar in the evening. Alcohol held me in its warm embrace on many nights when I went to bed, numbing me to emotional pain related to my divorce, and trauma from childhood.

Such is the shell game of self-deception that comes with bad habits and addiction, that when I traveled to Peru the idea of ending my alcohol dependency wasn't even on my list of goals. I simply didn't view it as a problem, though subconsciously I knew things had to change.

In the months of January, February and beyond after my return, I was hardly drawn to alcohol. I recall buying a small bottle of rye whisky, and wondering on the first sip why I'd ever liked this drink so much.

My addiction had evaporated like rain on Georgia asphalt. I was liberated from the underlying pain and PTSD that had motivated me to numb myself. (To actually numb my *Self*.)

I was a mostly-healed person now. I was free.

I could no longer rationalize my job. I'd thought to stay in it until both my sons were at least out of high school, if not university, but now I had to quit. Though it would take a year to do so, the die was cast for me to leave my 25-year career in business magazine journalism, and pursue new interests.

I continued meeting deadlines and writing my editorials like before, but my heart wasn't in it. The small talk and industry chat at conferences frustrated me. There was a world in need of saving! All the discussion of incremental change just didn't cut it anymore.

Like a ball of yarn rolling down a long staircase, the superstitions that govern people unraveled in my mind more and more each day.

Past work I'd done on this front — superstitions — accelerated. Buddhist teachings felt more real and alive than in the past, when I'd discovered them in books. Concepts of measured time, *work* deadlines, having a *boss*, ideas of *money*, even of *past and future* began to dissolve.

Had it not been for the need for me to provide for my children and be a good father, there's a chance — I think — that I'd have sold all my possessions and bought a one-way ticket to India. The thought of becoming a wandering *sadhu* tempted me.

I often thought about the floor of that bathroom stall, which had become an ice-covered stream, and realized more and more each day that mundane reality is a construct. I trusted it less and less each day.

There was no denying I was now *Guy Crittenden 2.0*. The new software contained fixes for many of the old bugs, and ran faster.

People remarked that there was something different about me, that I'd changed. I was less reactive to situations, slow to anger, and in general more compassionate.

I no longer manifested the selfish *wetiko* about which indigenous people rightfully complain.

The medicine had decolonized my mind.

* * *

To monitor and cope with the changes taking place inside me, I started a spiritual diary, which soon ran to hundreds of pages.

There was so much to record... so many changes!

In this offline account I wrote out detailed descriptions of strange experiences that appeared spontaneously and without the use of any hallucinogens.

I'd assumed when I returned from Peru that I'd possibly never drink ayahuasca again, though I hadn't given it much thought.

Coming home to Canada I'd initially felt the gateway to a magical kingdom closing. Yet I wasn't to pine for that kingdom for long; it soon thrust itself upon me.

I was surprised (to say the least) when about six weeks after my return from Peru, as I lay in bed in total darkness at about 4:00 a.m. one morning, I experienced the red and green ayahuasca pattern with almost the same intensity as if I'd drunk the medicine!

The imagery persisted for about an hour. I literally *couldn't believe my eyes* and pinched myself to make sure I wasn't dreaming. As when using the medicine, the pattern was equally visible whether my eyes were open or shut.

I wondered if this was some kind of flashback, and was amused and a bit frightened when it happened again the next morning, and then the next.

Have I damaged my brain? I wondered. *What on earth is going on?*

I conducted some research online and joined several Facebook discussion groups where modern-day shamans compare notes on all things related to the ancient mystical craft. I posted questions on ayahuasca discussion groups, too.

Has anyone else experienced this? I asked. *How common is it?*

It didn't take long for more experienced people to contact me and offer considerate advice. A common theme was that my kundalini energy was rising, along with the opening of my Third Eye.

I began to cautiously embrace the new journey, though I remained nervous about the strange phenomena that appeared with increasing frequency.

Nothing in my upbringing or cultural conditioning had prepared me for this. It's true to say, in fact, that school and work had bleached and vaccinated these phenomena out of my being.

I came to call my early morning spontaneous psychedelic experiences as *journeying* and, instead of resisting them, enhanced them by wearing a black eye mask, to extend the darkness past the time when sunlight slowly filtered into my bedroom. I later learned that *journeying* is the very word most shamans use to describe their travels in non-material reality.

In addition to the red and green ayahuasca pattern, I also began to experience *clouds of light*.

I wrestled with whether these were simply visual phenomena or, as I suspected, encounters with the universal consciousness seeping back into my awareness.

I developed the ability to summon, sometimes at will, a white light that started at the edge of my visual field and eventually filled it entirely. When this happened I felt completely topped up with subtle spiritual energy. A friend of mine well versed in these matters suggested this was a kind of crown chakra energy.

Even more strange was something I came to call the *disruption phenomenon*. This is tricky to describe, but was essentially a rapidly changing set of wildly different patterns and shapes that occupied about a third of the visual plane, directly in front of me.

This boiling pot of imagery was intriguing but also a bit frightening. I worried that if my consciousness somehow fell fully into it, I'd pass through a rip in the space/time continuum. Or that I'd go mad.

Much later I would conclude, when working with other plant medicines, that the disruption phenomenon might be my glimpsing the *transcendental object at the end of time*, to use Terence McKenna's memorable phrase, though it took many months for me to entertain this possibility.

A hallmark of this rapidly changing visual phenomenon was that it exuded an intelligence. It reminded me of the rectangular obelisk in Stanley Kubrick's film *2001: A Space Odyssey*. It had that same mysterious foreboding and omniscient quality, though its presentation to me was colorful and dynamic.

Other phenomena that began to appear were fully articulated and detailed hallucinatory landscapes that were as realistic as standing before an actual vista.

One example was a riverside landscape that reminded me of Ireland or medieval Europe. This place appeared more than once and was amazingly detailed. I could inspect every leaf on every tree, focus on the ripples in the flowing water, or the houses on the opposite bank.

I came to think of this as remote viewing. It didn't feel like a dream at all, and I was awake whenever it happened.

I also began experiencing lucid dreams, especially ones that involved tornadoes. I would wake up inside a dream in the manner presented in the film *Inception*. I would then work at remaining conscious about was happening in the dream, without waking into ordinary reality.

The tornadoes would appear in different guises. One time it was a great brown twister made of dust and sand that I intuited was in the Middle East somewhere. Another time a tornado loomed toward me as I stood at the edge of a great city. It was nighttime and the tornado was made of ice particles, lit up white from the lights of the city below. Yet another time it was a tornado of inky-black dust roaring across the

Great Plains of the United States, with me standing before it in utter astonishment.

In time I interpreted this as the Divine appearing to me as the whirlwind, just as described in the Book of Job in the Old Testament, and re-interpreted by the English poet and illustrator William Blake.

But nothing compared in its strangeness with the appearance on a regular basis of what I came to know as my *spirit animal*. This was a phenomenon I'd never even heard of before.

I began receiving almost daily visits from this creature, the body of which was composed of bright white light and deep black markings. I'd been advised by shamans that the relationship with such beings is tenuous and it's best not to name the animal or discuss it with others. But in later ayahuasca ceremonies I learned of my role as a communicator so I feel compelled to share my experience.

It appeared in a kind of undulating S or C shape, with the white parts made up of light as bright as a welder's arc, and triangular markings as black as night.

This creature appeared during the middle of the day or at almost any hour, starting as a tiny point of intense light that typically made it difficult — and then impossible — to ignore as it interrupted my ability to read text on my laptop screen, or drive a car.

The point of light would get larger and larger, and become fully recognizable as *a snake*.

Eventually the apparition filled most of my visual plane, then seemed to float over my head and shoulders. It moved somewhat like the real animal in our world but also had a symbolic look to it, like Navaho or Haida artwork.

Much later I came to interpret it as Pachamama, as presented in her serpent manifestations. This supreme deity in the cosmology of the Quechua people of the Peruvian highlands (direct descendants of the Inca) has three aspects: the sky (Wayramama), earth (Sachamama) and water (Yukamama).

I would later feel compelled to incorporate this spirit animal directly on my body in the form of an elaborate tattoo.

What is the message of these visitations? I wondered. *What is this strange animal trying to tell me?*

I was stumped.

Yet this creature had been given to me — *the sacred anaconda* — during one of the ayahuasca ceremonies in Peru.

I had forgotten.

It gradually dawned on me that there was no returning to my old unawakened state of being. Though I resisted, the shamanic realms were calling me back, whether I liked it or not. That life was over, and a new one had begun.

In time I sought opportunities to drink ayahuasca again, in Canada. I searched online for nearby meet-up groups and took advantage of some networking opportunities presented by a local association. I eventually found a person (several actually) who offered ayahuasca ceremonies in the vicinity of Toronto, Ontario.

Though such ceremonies aren't technically legal, it seemed that local law enforcement largely ignored the underground phenomenon of their being held. The police appeared to be preoccupied with the billion-dollar market in illegal and addictive narcotics.

I contacted a local facilitator and was eventually invited to a ceremony within an hour's drive of where I lived. As the weekend of that ceremony approached, my excitement grew.

I observed the ayahuasca diet and other preparations during the week before.

CEREMONY FOUR

My fourth ayahuasca ceremony took place in a large room at a rural retreat facility. The room was tightly packed with almost two dozen people: these included two female ayahuasceras (one of whom led the proceedings) and two participants who assisted with practical matters.

All of them drank the medicine, as is customary. I use the term *ayahuascera* (male form *ayahuascero*) to describe a facilitator who is sufficiently trained to serve the ayahuasca medicine and hold space for ceremony participants. Typically such a person will have served an apprenticeship of six months to two years with a curandero in South America, know how to prepare and cook the psychedelic brew, and deal with the most common issues that might surface during a ceremony (e.g., a person having a difficult night, or someone in need of First Aid). An ayahuascera should possess icaros (medicine songs) and know how to play or work with drums, leaf rattles and other instruments. Their role includes guiding the night with music and sound. This level of training is different than that of a curandero like Nihue Rao's Ricardo Amaringo. Such men and women have studied for many years or decades. They know how to heal with hundreds of different medicinal plants, and they more intensively use shamanic techniques during ceremony to affect and heal participants.

The holding of space by less experienced ayahuasceras, especially outside of South America, is controversial. Some people prefer to only sit with full-fledged curanderos, who sometimes hold ceremonies in North America and Europe to fund their operations down south. It's a personal choice.

I chose to sit with ayahuasceras in order to access the medicine in Canada. I was aware of the risks, especially after my venomization in Peru by spirit-world spiders. I chose to accept those risks and step into what became a more mature relationship with the medicine.

The lead ayahuascera — Natasha — had a good reputation and had been trained in traditional methods in the Amazon. She spent time there each year working with a shaman in the jungle, and pulling in more icaros.

I decided to go for it.

Natasha had a beautiful singing voice, and put on an excellent ceremony (as I would find) with wonderful medicine songs, hand drumming and other elements.

The assistant facilitator was from Quebec and normally led mushroom ceremonies. She remarked that she travels to Mexico for the Sun Dance and the Moon Dance.

As per usual, the ceremony took place at night. Everyone gathered in the early evening after fasting that afternoon. Before the ceremony, for about two hours, people had the chance to settle in and casually converse.

One person had brought a deck of prophecy cards, which some of us took turns pulling. I shuffled the deck and decided that although

I'd been skeptical of these things in the past, I'd take it seriously this evening. Hadn't my mind already been opened to some pretty unusual things already?

I resolved that whatever card I pulled, I'd take it as an omen. Interestingly, I pulled the Shaman card. Intriguing indeed.

At 9:00 pm the formal ceremony began, beginning with each person sharing their *intention* for the evening.

Each person spoke aloud to the group from their mat for about two to four minutes. As per usual, I was impressed that intentions varied as greatly as the number of people there; they included such things as one person wanting fresh insights into how to overcome her long-standing depression issues. Another person sought relief from a chronic illness, while another hoped to deepen her recovery from drug addiction. One young businessperson sought further insights into managing people and creating a team in their place of work.

There were many other intentions.

The intention I set for myself was to more deeply understand the phenomena I'd recently experienced involving the visions of geometric patterns, white or colored lights, hallucinatory landscapes and (especially) the visits from the spirit animal.

The ayahuasceras walked around the room and used a feather to wave flower-scented tobacco onto each participant — smudging them — and then called us one at a time to come to the front of the room and drink.

Natasha indicated there were three bottles of ayahuasca on hand and that she would choose which brew to offer each person. None was necessarily better than the other, she said.

I asked for a small cup, as I'd earlier told the facilitator I wasn't seeking a *big* experience that evening, only a subtle reconnection to La Madre.

The ayahuascera poured a smallish amount into the cup. I knelt and drank it back, noticing the awful taste and wretched feeling as the sticky brown liquid hit my empty stomach. Blech!

After we drank, Natasha said good night and pinched out the two candles beside her, plunging the room into darkness. The only light that remained was a bit of faint moonlight that filtered through the edge of the room's large windows, which were covered with black cloth.

In the darkness I crawled over to a young man seated across from me who was drinking ayahuasca for the first time.

Good luck tonight on your journey! I said to him, while exchanging a fist handshake.

This is something that Dan Cleland had done for me during my first-ever ceremony and I'd appreciated it.

I sat on my mat for about 40 minutes before feeling a faint effect from the medicine, but over time I realized the brew I'd been served was having virtually no impact.

Since my experiences in Peru had been so big, and the last one so terrifying, I felt some relief about this. I considered just leaving it at that for the night.

I later learned that this ayahuascera, out of caution, normally serves only a very mild brew to people who drink with her for the first time.

Despite being quite sober I enjoyed listening to the sounds of people experiencing the medicine, which included vomiting, and also the icaros which Natasha delivered with verve and talent. She was sometimes accompanied by the second facilitator.

The icaros were quite different from the songs I'd heard in Peru, which had all been in Spanish or the Shipibo language. Some of this woman's songs were in English, and many were accompanied by a drum, a rattle or a small harmonium. Her voice, and that of her co-pilot, was exquisite.

In one corner a woman sobbed. On the other side of the room someone laughed a little. Now and again someone would purge and I found this sound pleasant and in no way offensive. I imagined the other person experiencing relief, and would sometimes pump my fist in the air to silently say, *Right on, sister!* or *Right on, brother!* Though they couldn't see me, I imagined they might pick up the gesture telepathically.

After a while Natasha took a break from her singing and joked in whispers with the other facilitator. I enjoyed the sense of fun the two women brought to the whole experience. I appreciated that these affairs don't have to be so deadly serious!

When Natasha called for interested parties to come for a second cup, I walked over to accept, again asking for a small amount.

She asked me what I thought of the first cup.

No effect, I answered.

She poured a small to medium amount of what I (correctly) surmised was a different brew. I can't remember whether it was at that moment or later that she told me this was an ayahuasca batch she'd cooked for an entire week. (Some brews are made over a 48-hour period or even just 24 hours).

This was my first introduction into the subtleties of ayahuasca craftsmanship.

After I swallowed the bitter medicine I lit up completely before I even walked the six or seven feet back to my mat. The hyperspace enveloped me and the visions came on strong. I was thankful to find my mat and settle in while this was even possible.

My bowels seemed settled and I didn't feel especially nauseous.

The higher octane medicine (that I later called *super test*) sent me on the biggest roller coaster ride of my life. The visions persisted intensely for about five hours. I was still journeying long after most of the other participants fell asleep in the wee hours of the morning. The intense visions almost surpassed anything I'd seen before, which is really saying something.

As expected, the first visions were the classic (for me) aya red and green pattern. The difference in this case was that the pattern started moving much sooner and quickly morphed into three-dimensional lines and grids that had a computer matrix feeling.

Things became brightly colored and three-dimensional, with crazy geometry and everything shape-shifting at a rapid pace. These things are impossible to describe sufficiently but an apt metaphor might be what the underwater world looked like to a microscopic creature during the Cambrian era, with hundreds of different animals moving about, appearing in vivid hues of blue, red, pink, magenta, violet, green and orange.

I'll never know fully how much of what developed related to the potency of the brew or my own sensitivity. Maybe I'd evolved a bit in the months since my Peru trip. But within perhaps 20 minutes I began to see visions that were more intense than anything I'd seen in South America.

As with some of the Peruvian visions, a lot of what I saw looked like the "CAD" armatures that computer animators develop for characters before they put on the "digital skin." This persisted for a while, but over the hours that followed this kind of imagery gave way to a far more full-blown 3D and realistic visionary experience.

The night was filled with a lot of carnival-type images. Faces. Clowns. Animals. 3D lines with thousands of tarantula eyes that drew themselves into complex rectangles and mandala forms.

Everything evolved itself in ceaseless motion and creativity.

If you or I hired the entire Walt Disney animation studio for a year and gave them a $50 million budget to create a complex, surreal animated film, what they'd produce might account for maybe just 10 minutes of what I saw and experienced continuously over five hours. This is not an exaggeration.

It was such an intense ride that, honestly, if the facilitators had come up to me after the first 20 minutes and told me they could stop it for a fee of $1,000, I would have written a check there and then. (Assuming I could hold the pen.)

There is no escape, I thought. *I simply have to ride it out.*

I spent most of the time reclining in a half-lying, half-sitting posture propped up on pillows. (Thankfully I had brought four from home.) At times I sat cross-legged and upright at the foot of my mat. Though I wished to lie down completely, there was no point: lying down made the visions even more overpowering and sinister, and ratcheted up my considerably growing feeling of nausea.

Eyes were a big theme this night. I was treated to a review — close up — of every kind of eye from among all the insects and animals and birds and fish that had ever lived on our planet.

I noted in all the eyes the universal consciousness looking out. Though they whizzed past me at a fast pace I could nevertheless make out the details of each eye, and note their particular beauty.

There were eyes from different kinds of gazelles and antelope and deer — a whole panoply of herbivores. There were predator eyes in rapid succession, including cheetahs, lions, tigers and hundreds of other big cats, including ones that no doubt lived in earlier times and were extinguished during the last Ice Age. There were thousands of insect eyes and spider eyes. Looking closely at spider eyes is not an experience I'd normally welcome, yet even in these I saw the universal consciousness gazing out.

This was no doubt a core teaching.

At another point I saw the evolution of human beings from apes through hominids to homo sapiens via a rapidly-changing 3D modeling of their heads and faces. It was like a National Geographic "Origins of Man" program on fast play: hundreds of different hominid types morphed in front of me and I had a sense of this not being a dream at all, but a scientific review. For those who have never drunk ayahuasca this will sound like madness, but I felt the representations were accurate in every respect and that I was being shown real information.

My memory is unreliable for certain parts of the journey: I experienced too much to recall and retell. Time doesn't function in a purely linear manner in hyperspace. One can experience hundreds of events in only an hour. And was that really an hour? Perhaps by some clock, but experientially it can feel like days.

Yet certain other episodes jump out that are important.

I encountered several new patterns I'd never encountered before through ayahuasca. One was like cobblestones, though perfectly flat, and another was like the fragmented pattern on the glazing of a very old porcelain jar. Imagery would appear either within these patterns or on the other side, as if I was viewing things through frosted or stained glass.

The pattern I enjoyed most had a very Gaelic vibe to it, though I can't logically say why. The pattern was of smooth dark stone (like jet) polished to a mirror finish, then bathed in firelight. The stones were each about the size of a small dinner plate, irregularly shaped but smooth in the way of cobblestones; they were perfectly flat but the edges were raised and polished.

I thought, *This would be a great texture for the opening credits of* Game of Thrones.

I thought the pattern might be dragon scales and this set in motion their morphing into a dragon that appeared from a kind of mist or fire. The dragon was incredibly detailed and beautiful and green.

I thought for a moment, *He's a variation on the snake.*

The dragon had a masculine energy. I concluded later that this dragon was definitely calling me back to my Irish and Celtic roots, and Celtic/Gaelic shamanism. My field notes record:

I know I must travel to Ireland to study this.

This theme came back several times.

Another major component of the evening was the experience of my spirit animal and integration with it.

I'd endured some dark visions, and then used a well-rehearsed technique of concentrating and pulling up white light with my eyes.

In previous journeying (not on ayahuasca) I had seen the edge of the spirit animal in the very lowest region of my visual field. I could call upon him to imbue my visual field with bright white light.

However, now, among dark visions, the spirit animal appeared to abandon me. I was really annoyed, and said so.

Hey, you visit me all those months and interrupt my day, I complained. *And now when I need you, you're nowhere to be found?*

Then an inner voice asked me, *Whose eyes are you looking through right now?*

This thought made the hairs on the back of my neck stand on end.

The realization hit me: The spirit animal is not *inside* me. It *is* me.

We are one and the same.

It was then that I realized the meaning of the daily visions I'd had over the previous six weeks or so, in which the animal slowly filled my visual field and made it impossible to work (like a classic migraine headache).

I'd misinterpreted it as *floating past me* over my shoulder and past my head. All along it had been working to show me (in the only way it could) that it had entered the top of my head (the crown chakra) and was part of me. Instead of "looking for it" to appear during my ayahuasca experience, I realized I "am" the animal.

As soon as the medicine saw that this was now clear to me, everything changed up.

I was then treated to a series of visions that taught me how to behave toward threats, by embracing my inner serpent.

Dark visions appeared again and again and I simply stared them down until they vanished. My spirit animal is a creature of which most other animals are afraid; simply taking a stand and embracing the mojo of this creature is enough to get the job done, at least most of the time.

I then received many lessons about this animal's life and attitude, which I realized I had to incorporate into my life. This includes allowing myself lots of downtime, unapologetic lingering and luxuriating in simply *being* and then taking action (e.g., hunting for food) when needed.

I gained confidence in the hyperspace from adopting this animal's attitude, its spirit, and I was taught telepathically that this would manifest in the regular world.

I suspect that what happened next related to my new spirit animal confidence.

A metaphor seems apt from first-person video gaming, where one's avatar is, say, an errant knight.

In the first stage of the game lots of scenarios are presented in which you learn to use your sword, shield and other weapons. You learn which buttons to push on the controller to master actions like ducking, jumping, stabbing, blocking and so on. You learn where to find healing potions to uplevel your "health" meter and you learn which kinds of people are allies or enemies. From there the adventure unfolds.

It was a bit like that as ayahuasca messed around with me, putting different situations in front of me so I could practice dealing with them.

Fairly quickly I realized how my attitude influences which way things go in my life. Often the visions took the form of terrifying animal and insect faces which would quickly morph into something humorous, like a carnival clown or cartoon image. At one point a whole array of frightening entities toggled back and forth between being terrifying and being the cast of Sesame Street (Oscar the Grouch, Big Bird, etc.).

It was really fun, and I appreciated the medicine's humor. She was sashaying with attitude herself, this night, in a way saying, *So, you know those images that frightened you so much in Peru? Let me show you how I make those!* And I got a kind of backstage tour of the magician's secrets, learning how the show works, with the main lesson being that they are illusions.

The universal consciousness can conjure up heaven or hell in an instant, depending on how we are in this dimension and this moment. It's a bit like a Kafka short story: that castle in the distance can be a fun amusement park if we want it to be, or it can be a sinister impediment that stops our life journey dead in its tracks.

In the end it's up to us. Our problem is that we take it all so *seriously*. It becomes high drama.

Why? Because in ordinary life we're immersed deeply in the illusion that this dimension is real and not simply the wondrous simulation that it is.

That night I came to understand the cosmic joke at which the laughing Buddha chortles. You and I and everything else are one, in this dimension and the next. No one and no thing actually dies. We're avatars in an eternal cosmic virtual reality.

The morphing crazy contusions of frightening and funny faces and images continued for what felt like hours. It was quite a tremendous show. Even if I hadn't received teachings from the visions, their beauty and complexity were worth the price of admission (i.e., nausea).

Later in the night — at last! — I managed to have a major purge, throwing up heavily into my bucket via a series of powerful heaves between which I could barely gasp for air.

To the non-initiated this must sound awful and reason enough not to drink ayahuasca, but for me it was a high point of the night and something I enjoyed greatly. I felt (as I'd read elsewhere) like I was throwing up all kinds of negative personal issues. It was purifying and I felt light and wonderful for days afterward.

Most blessedly, this purge freed me permanently from experiencing the nausea I'd felt in ceremonies up to this point. I was (thankfully) able to enjoy the rest of the night's visions free of that suffering.

The final big ticket item was a series of lessons about my own narcissism. In these I was shown over and over how, despite thinking I'm humble, I continue to put myself first, not community or nature. There were several major smackdowns that felt like they were delivered from the hand of a kind but formidable mother.

The medicine pointed out that I was here, attending this ceremony, for my own selfish reasons, when I knew perfectly well that my stepmother was dying.

Why aren't you at her side? La Madre asked.

Just before this point in the night I'd decided that the overall roller coaster ride had been enough, and I'd decided not to return for the second ceremony the next evening.

Or so I thought.

After a few lessons about my narcissism I then concluded I had to return even if I didn't drink aya, to at least be of service to the other ceremony participants.

Heck, I thought, *I could sit in the corner and help guide people to the washroom with a red flashlight, if I was sober.*

But ayahuasca smacked me down over that idea too, showing me how pathetic it was.

Is that all you can think of when your stepmother is dying? she asked. I was then reminded of many vignettes from my childhood, and my stepmother's many acts of kindness toward me.

My stepmother Carol had become reclusive from me and the rest of our family after my father died about 18 years before. She hadn't kept in touch much and my only contact with her over the years was an email here or there, or a phone call at Christmas (usually initiated by me). Once in a while I'd meet her at a coffee shop in Orillia, near where she lived on a farm property. This contact was always my idea.

Carol rarely asked about my children or took much interest in my life. I met with her mostly because I felt sorry for her: she was a former alcoholic who stopped drinking years ago but never replaced alcohol with any kind of spirituality or uplifting practice. She was simply an alcoholic without the booze, white-knuckling it through life. She lived with a common law partner who discouraged her from engaging with the rest of the family or friends. It was all very sad.

My stepmother had contracted a form of terminal COPD illness a couple of years ago that left her short of breath and unable to perform anything more than simple tasks. She'd become bedridden a few months before, and then, just days before this ceremony, had taken a turn for the worse.

I'd visited her in hospital about a month before (thankfully) when she was taken there by ambulance for treatment of an infection. A tall woman who at one point stood 5'10" in her stocking feet, Carol was down to 87 pounds. She looked like a concentration camp survivor. I believed the hospital visit would be the last time I'd see her. She was also a hoarder (just like on the TV shows) and I'd been told her house was a disaster.

Between that and the knowledge that her boyfriend was already caring for her, I had felt okay about not visiting.

Ayahuasca showed me how inadequate this was, how pathetic my excuses and rationalizations were, and how much more I could be doing. It was clear I should have canceled my attendance at the ayahuasca retreat when I heard the news about her downturn, and should have gone much further outside my comfort zone to be of assistance.

Damn! I felt shame for being such a narrow person and resolved that I'd attend to her house come hell or high water the next night. And I felt relieved that I wouldn't have to suffer another rocketship ride on ayahuasca either, if I missed the Saturday night ceremony.

At this point I felt a curious surge of empathy from the ayahuasca spirit.

She knew that I understood the lesson, and things were left a bit ambiguous. I was assured that a place had been prepared in the afterlife for my stepmother, who would embark on another journey.

The lesson became contrarian: I should not fret too much; the universe was ready for her.

Eventually the ceremony concluded. I'm not sure at what time as my sense of such things was skewed. I had walked out to use the bathroom in the middle of the night and had found I could barely stand. I was still intoxicated. I had to hold the walls with my hands like an astronaut navigating his way down a corridor in the International Space Station.

It may have been about 3:00 am when the ceremony concluded and the ayahuasceras walked around to each participant and blew sacred tobacco smoke, first on their heads, then their cupped hands, and then into their chests.

I lay on my mat for hours, awake, listening to the gentle pulsing music that Natasha left playing over a stereo. It was quiet enough that those who could sleep slept, but I remained awake with visions until the sun rose.

And yet in the morning, despite not really sleeping, I had great energy.

As is the tradition, we sat again as a group at about 8:00 am for *la conversación*. Each person took a few minutes to describe their experiences, not dwelling too much on the details of visions but, at the facilitator's request, talking about the main conclusions they drew from their experiences. Again I was struck by the breathtaking variety of learnings and healing modalities. Some people had had rough nights and tough experiences. The medicine had kicked their asses and made them face their shit. Others had gentle experiences, all light and kindness.

Everyone viewed their problems and challenges from new angles, and felt empowered to take these on with fresh insight and vigor.

I summarized my experiences briefly and announced that, given the intensity of the whole thing, I would likely not return again the following night. I would try to visit my dying stepmother.

We rose and enjoyed breakfast together as a group, grazing from an assortment of fruit dishes and nuts and other healthy vegan items brought by participants. I was grateful for a large cup of strong coffee that Natasha brewed after grinding fresh beans with an enormous stone post and mortar.

This was a brew from her hands that I could actually enjoy the taste of!

Importantly, Natasha implored me to stay for the second ceremony, which would take place that night. She gently explained that I had a lot of integration work to do.

You shouldn't go back to the world with that door wide open, she said. She conveyed that the open door was a holdover from my Peru trip.

We need to create a container for that energy, she said.

Something intuitive inside me told me to listen to her, and not rush off to be with my stepmother. It felt like the universe was intervening through Natasha. I had understood the lesson in responsibility and compassion from the night before, and now the universe was speaking to me, asking me to stay put, to aid in healing and, possibly, even to prevent injury.

I felt it wise to listen to Natasha, so I left my mat and other belongings on the floor, and didn't pack up my car. I decided I would return that evening for the second ceremony.

I drove off to run some errands. These included buying flashlights for people who had forgotten theirs, and transparent red tape with which to cover the ends.

I'd spent the night in a high-traffic area and had been stepped upon a few times by people who lacked flashlights of their own. This it was an investment in my own safety as well as an act of minor generosity!

The hieroglyphic word *herw* is commonly paired with the word *ma'a*, "truth," as the noble goal of life: one strives at death to have accomplished *ma'a herw*, not to speak the truth or have a true voice but to be true to the clean underlying pattern of what is, the *ma'a herw* — *the true vibration, the vibration of truth.*

— SUSAN BRIND MORROW, *The Dawning Moon of the Mind: Unlocking the Pyramid Texts*

Later that afternoon I returned to the property with some flashlights and red tape, and sat in the kitchen affixing small pieces of the tape to them. This was to dim their light. Ayahuasca makes one's eyesight and hearing especially sensitive. Anything like a normal lantern offends the eyes, and one can hear people whispering from across the room as if they're only inches away. I planned to hand out the flashlights to anyone who forgot theirs.

The main room where the ceremony was to be conducted was quite small for the number of people in attendance. There were no lights in the hallway, and the second washroom was upstairs. I was afraid someone might fall down them.

As people arrived, I made small talk and handed out flashlights here and there. By the time ceremony approached, the room filled up again, and I alternated between lying back and resting, and talking to people. Most were repeat visitors from the night before, but there were a few new faces. A couple had flown in from New York: it was to be their first ceremony.

It seemed like the breakdown was roughly even between men and women, most of whom were in their twenties or early thirties.

This time, having stayed from the night before, I was able to pick a safer position in the room for my mat and pillows, but I was still in a high-traffic area. I set down an empty plastic yoghurt container beside my mat that would serve, if needed, as a purge bucket. Beside that I placed a small woven shoulder bag decorated with intricate and color-ful Shipibo designs that I'd bought in Peru. In this bag I'd placed a few items of use in ceremony, namely my flashlight and a small roll of toilet paper — must-have items in case I needed to use the bathroom in a hurry.

This is where I also stored my car keys and (turned off) cell phone. I'd learned from the previous night's ceremony that it's useful having one's valuables in one place. (I'd locked my wallet in the car.)

I felt the usual sense of excitement and foreboding as the shadows grew longer and the sun began to set.

My thoughts meandered back to the ceremonies in Peru. It had been much more enigmatic — compared to this place — out in the jungle, with the call of birds and frogs at night, the looming interior roof of the maloka with its wagon-wheel network of beams and trusses, and the curanderos' faces lit up faintly by candle light.

I remembered my venomization by spirit-world spiders. Had that been real? And if so, in what sense? Could I actually have died, had the curandero not intervened?

I thought so. I was weak back then. I was probably weak now. I was untrained and had been unprepared for the risk of *actual death* on the hero's journey. This was no Joseph Campbell essay: ayahuasca could function as a sweet medicine lifting one up to angelic realms, but it can also access demonic energies.

My encounter with spirit-world spider energies had been like an ordeal poison, of the kind used by some tribes for initiation. I wondered if I hadn't misinterpreted the whole thing. Maybe the curandero Amaringo was wrong; instead of my having dragged something sinister into the maloka from outside, perhaps the spiders had instigated a shamanic death — something sought out by adepts. It certainly felt like I died over and over, and came back gasping for air, fighting for my life.

I'd always feared spiders. Maybe I'd had a bad history with them in a previous life, assuming reincarnation is real. Maybe I'd even *been* one, or had been eaten by one...

And then there was the lesson of the mother, with the whole maloka rocking back and forth, taking me inside my mother's womb. Had that been a hallucination? Or a memory? It seemed like the latter, but how? How did the plant achieve that? Lasting memories aren't laid down until much later in childhood.

I thought about my stepmother Carol's impending death. When would it arrive? And should I be at her side?

I'd thought about it all day. Her common law second husband — a younger man (my own age) — was living with her and was said to be notoriously difficult. I wouldn't be welcome there. In fact, it might not only be awkward, but dangerous. I'd have trouble finding the place, and then what would I do?

The medicine had opened my heart the night before. It had shown me the emotions I should be feeling and acknowledging. It was pushing me to be fully human, fully realized. It was irrational, this thought of driving there to be with her. But still, was I making an error, staying here for this ayahuasca ceremony?

I felt conflicted. Part of me wanted to go, and yet Natasha had asked me — almost *told* me — to remain.

And so I chose to stay and place my trust in this strange process.

CEREMONY FIVE

This evening I was about to learn about the other side of ayahuasca — her gentle side, her subtlety.

I was also to benefit from another component of the medicine that has caused me to believe its future in North America and around the globe may be different than that of, say, LSD in the 1970s.

And that is the component of *shamanism*.

Allan Watts once remarked that the problem with LSD (about which he was otherwise enthusiastic) was its not being accompanied by any kind of discipline. Eastern cultures, he said, understood the rigors of mystical reality and instilled practices to manage the experiences, from seated meditation to martial arts, yoga, breath work and artistic rituals.

The culture of dropping acid and partying, Watts warned, would bring about the very circumstances the authorities would use to justify shutting down the whole party. Which is exactly what happened.

The evening of my fifth ayahuasca ceremony was not so much about the medicine itself as it was about the shamanic dimension.

The ayahuasceras entered the room, set up their leaf rattles and feathers and other instruments, and the expected plastic bottles filled with brown ayahuasca liquid, and used some sage to smudge the space.

The ceremony began at 9:00 p.m. with the sharing of intentions, tobacco smudging of each person, and the quenching of candles.

For this evening I set my intention toward integration of the previous night's teachings and experiences.

As with the first night, my first cup was small and the experiences were light. Unlike the first night, however, this was not because the visions were absent: instead, they were simply very subtle. I had to work hard to see things, but they were there. I was a bit dissatisfied with not seeing more, but thankful to not feel ill or overwhelmed. I chose to use this time to take in the room and feel kinship with the "tribe" of spiritual wanderers inside the sacred space.

I accepted Natasha's invitation when she offered a second cup. She again started to pour me a small cup. I was wary: a small cup had sent me on a rocketship ride the night before.

Sensing my hesitation, she poured a very tiny amount. I drank this, deliberately leaving a bit in the cup.

I was playing it safe this night.

This turned out to be the Goldilocks portion for me: not too much and not too little. The visions came on and were strong, yet also subtle.

I found this a wonderful place to be: I was able to contemplate and reflect on what I saw without being overwhelmed.

I saw many of the same things as the night before, but with more time intervals in between. I was now able to appreciate each tableau or pattern.

Was this a better approach with the medicine, going forward? I wondered. *Can I regulate my experience?*

I'm becoming a more seasoned aya drinker, I thought to myself in the darkness. *I don't need the crazy-ass ride but instead this more paced experience...*

The visions were indeed stunning, and detailed beyond belief.

At times I felt like a clergyman walking through a great cathedral when it's not in service. I had a chance to reflect on the ceiling murals without the crowds and distractions, or inspect the intricate filigree woodwork of the pews and altar up close.

I saw the green and red aya pattern, and realized how inadequate my earlier attempts were to describe it as the outlines of "noodles in a bowl." Word descriptions will always be a poor substitute for the actual experience. Descriptions are like trying to render the Mona Lisa in crayon.

Again I saw many patterns, and vistas of eyes. On this night the eyes appeared one at a time so I could inspect their beauty s-l-o-w-l-y. So many different kinds of eyes from different animals and insects and other beings! Sad horse and deer eyes. Pensive elephant eyes. Tense insect and spider eyes.

Each eye radiated the consciousness of God looking out.

Again that was the lesson.

And again I saw terrifying faces and images that modulated quickly into positive or funny. Ayahuasca showed me over and over that this is all part of the great Cosmic Joke. (Apparently, as with a child, she'd surmised that I learn best via lots of repetition.)

The pattern of burnished "jet" stone with the mirror finish appeared: Dragon scales. This evening I had more time to look at them and ponder their mysterious meaning.

Unfortunately this vision was interrupted by one of many unwanted distractions that night.

Some people forgot to put their flashlights under their clothes (to dim the light further). Some stumbled over me on their way to the bathroom. I recall thinking I must get to these events earlier and claim a better spot!

One person made blowing sounds most of the night that annoyed me, or sang for long periods with the facilitators, out of rhythm and out of tune at times. I put up with this for a long time out of respect for whatever he was going through, but eventually asked Natasha to kindly ask him to cut it out: his actions were interfering with my experience. He quieted down and I was able to go back to enjoying the icaros.

Then someone fell quite noisily in the hallway, pulling me out of my visions.

There were lots of sounds from people vomiting. I considered this positive and found, ironically, that these sounds brought my concentration back into the visions.

For some duration of the ceremony I thought about my stepmother, lying in bed at home slowly shuffling off this mortal coil. I felt the need to tell her that it was alright to die.

You can let go, Carol, I said out loud. *A place has been prepared for you on the other side. It's safe. I've seen it!*

This is only one of thousands of lives you're going to live! New adventures await you!

Carol... Am I really in contact with you? I thought to myself.

There was a *knowing* that this was the case. The plant medicine had put my consciousness on another frequency: one that transcends time and space. It was telepathic in a way that reminded me of my father Max's passing about two decades earlier when I was just 35.

* * *

My father had come out of decades of remission with multiple sclerosis, about a decade before he died. My dad sat down on the couch one day and couldn't stand up — thus began a gradual descent, which started with him using a cane to walk, then getting around in a mechanized scooter-style wheelchair. I have many memories of meeting my father in restaurants, with him showing up on his scooter, and using his cane (and some help from me) to transfer in and out of a regular chair.

Eventually he couldn't transfer his weight at all and had to use a hospital-style wheelchair, pushed by other people. Then that was too much, and in his late fifties he spent his days in a hospital-style bed set up in his apartment. The mattress was inflated constantly by a pump, designed to prevent bedsores. It worked imperfectly.

Gradually Max's ability to do anything declined further. MS is such a cruel disease, and you never know what part of your nervous system is going to fail next, and whether or not the change will be permanent.

For a few months my dad went blind, but then his sight came back. He had a lifelong dread of being quadriplegic, and eventually lost the use of his limbs, except for limited use of his right forearm and hand, which allowed him to smoke.

In what would be his final weeks, he lost the ability to chew food or swallow properly. The doctor suggested that my stepmother grind his food in a blender and serve it to him with a straw. I couldn't blame my dad for beginning to give up at that point. Increasingly there was a far-away look in his eyes.

One Sunday evening Carol called me to say my father had been taken (yet again) to hospital after (yet again) he stopped breathing and was revived.

You might want to call him in the morning, she said. *I'm sure he'd love to hear from you.*

That night I had the strangest dreams, lucid almost. I felt my father's mind reaching across the ether to talk to me. He was trying to tell me something. I tossed and turned.

The next morning I called him at the hospital after arriving at work. The hospital switchboard put me through to his room, where a nurse answered.

We're busy trying to revive him, the nurse said. *He stopped breathing a while ago.*

Oh, I said. *How long has it been since he breathed last?*

About five minutes, the nurse answered.

I paused and turned this around in my mind for a few seconds.

So you're telling me he's dead, I stated more than asked.

Yes, the nurse answered, awkwardly. *I think so.*

I had called my father at the moment of his death, it turned out. I'd narrowly missed my chance for one last conversation.

The one he'd reached out for, in the realm of dreams...

* * *

After thinking for a long time about Carol I thought I'd cheat a bit and sleep for some of the night, as my dose was not strong. But the opposite happened. The dose was so perfect I spent almost the whole night sitting upright, happily awake, often at the end of my mat participating in songs (when asked) or chanting.

I felt truly connected to the ayahuasceras and enjoyed their laughter. I enjoyed several hours of journeying — so magical! And without nausea! I sat on my mat in the dark, a traveler on the shoreline of a Leviathan sea of consciousness, at the edge of a universe glittering with stars.

It was a special time far away from the workaday world in which we spend so much of our precious lives.

In the early morning hours I drifted off to sleep, listening to a wonderful soundtrack the facilitators played through a stereo, after the ceremony was formally closed.

I slept in the fetal position for a long time.

During formal conversation and sharing the next morning I was interested in the stories of the other participants, all so different and intriguing.

I told the group about my night and how gratifying it was to go beyond the "big cosmic lessons" and into more subtle terrain. I was thankful to ayahuasca for sorting out my personal issues; while I had much more to learn about myself I felt she got me focused on community and healing the planet. I told them about my interaction with Carol, and what I'd told her telepathically.

After a breakfast of organic snacks I packed up my belongings and said my goodbyes to the group. Almost everyone offered an embrace.

Good luck, brother, was said to me many times, as well as *happy journeying* and *I look forward to seeing you at the next gathering.*

I sat in the car in the bright sunlight of the spring morning and thought to check the email messages on my phone. I powered it up, then saw a flurry of emails concerning my stepmother.

She had died that night.

* * *

Just three days after the ceremony I was visited again by my spirit animal. It appeared as per usual from a tiny point of light in the distance and gradually floated closer and closer and then disappeared into the top of my head.

Except there was a difference this time: Instead of being made only of white light with black markings it vibrated and shimmered with tints of different brilliant colors, red, green, orange, yellow, pink... It was transformed, as no doubt I was too.

The afternoon I returned home, my girlfriend at the time described an experience she had during the night when I was in ceremony. One of my visions had been of integrating more with my spirit animal — something I hadn't mentioned to her.

She had woken up in the middle of the night, in the thrall of a physical interaction with an unseen force that caused her distress. She'd felt her body had been squeezed, as if in the coils of a constrictor. It appeared the energy of the spirit animal (me) had reached through the night a great distance and engaged in this bizarre contact.

I must have appeared ashen-faced when she told me.

Days later a shaman friend wrote me an interesting note after reading my account, which I'd posted online. He said his animal also comes from that "point of light." He wrote:

> The light sometimes called the star is actually the sushumna, the spiritual channel of the spine which goes up to the Third Eye and extends out into the universe.

He recommended that I tell my animal I love it, dance it, let it experience through me.

Learn its body language and ways of communication, he wrote, noting that he thought his animal was saying "no" until he learned that shaking the head was part of a friendly approach.

I followed his advice.

We have to create culture. Don't watch TV, don't read magazines, don't even listen to NPR. Create your own roadshow. The nexus of space and time where you are now is the most immediate sector of your universe, and if you're worrying about Michael Jackson or Bill Clinton or somebody else, then you are disempowered, you're giving it all away to icons, icons which are maintained by an electronic media so that you want to dress like X or have lips like Y. This is shit-brained, this kind of thinking. That is all cultural diversion, and what is real is you and your friends and your associations, your highs, your orgasms, your hopes, your plans, your fears. And we are told "no," we're unimportant, we're peripheral. "Get a degree, get a job, get a this, get a that." And then you're a player. You don't want to even play in that game. You want to reclaim your mind and get it out of the hands of the cultural engineers who want to turn you into a half-baked moron consuming all this trash that's being manufactured out of the bones of a dying world.

— Terence McKenna

My belief in a conventional materialist reality was shaken most, perhaps, by the three times I almost died in Brazil in 1984. Though I ignored or partially suppressed the information from my mind and simply "got on with living," I was haunted over the years by the triplicate of strange coincidences that corroded my otherwise stridently atheist, empiricist mental outlook.

I traveled to Rio de Janeiro in November of the year Orwell made famous and immersed myself in the vibrant local culture. I avoided other tourists during my six weeks there, socializing instead with locals while living in a rented apartment three blocks from the famous Copacabana Beach. I took Portuguese lessons daily, and partied hard with the *cariocas*. Many of the young Brazilian women were as attractive as the ones in films I first encountered from that country in the 1970s like *Bye Bye Brazil*, and I caught a taste of what it might feel like to be a rock star: my blonde hair and pale skin drew attention. Women rightly assumed I was a foreigner and wrongly hoped I might be their ticket to a better life in North America. I was propositioned regularly, even once on the bus. Their interest in escape was spurred by the collapsing economy; triple-digit inflation caused the government not only to devalue the currency while I was there, but to replace the *cruzeiro* with the *cruzado*.

In addition to sensuous tourism my trip had an overarching purpose. I'd been listless since university and the stall of an attempted visual art career. I was toying with the notion of becoming a photojournalist, to profitably repurpose my overdeveloped visual sensibility. To that end, I planned to visit the *favelas* (slums) of Rio and produce a photo essay of whatever I discovered there.

I made some full-day trips into the favelas, accompanied by armed guards whom I recruited at the military police station at the bottom of the mountain. The $20 per day I paid them in US dollars likely equaled a week or even a month's pay. I entered the favelas with a hired car and driver, and the guards followed in their vehicle, semiautomatic rifles at the ready.

I had many adventures in those slums perched high on the sugarloaf shaped mountains and obtained some stunning photos, but the relevant story here is the time my driver and I somehow got too far ahead of the guards and came to a fork in the road.

Should I go to the right or left? the driver asked.

I intuited that we should go left, and gave that instruction. The driver roared up that road to the very top of the mountain and stopped in a less dense area that was relatively flat. My driver and I stepped out of the car and I passed the time waiting for the guards by taking photos of some very beautiful young girls around the age of 10 who came out to investigate us from inside a large dormitory-style building.

My driver explained that the girls were orphans and the property of a local gang, which housed and fed them in this facility until they were old enough to work in the city's brothels.

A few minutes later my guards pulled up and jumped out of their car. They agitatedly jabbered at me in Portuguese until I asked them to please slow down. They'd seen my car idling at the fork in the road and were greatly relieved when we chose the road to the left, as the right road was most definitely the wrong road. It was called *a boca da serpente* (the mouth of the serpent), because whoever or whatever went down it was never seen again. The road apparently led through a cluster of buildings controlled by a drug gang with whom these policemen and their brothers-in-arms had been fighting an ongoing gun battle for months — and losing. Had I instructed my driver to turn down that path, within minutes the wheels of our car would have been shot out, and we'd have been executed for our meagre possessions, with the car later chopped up for parts. In a best-case scenario I might have been kidnapped, with my ear mailed to my family for ransom.

The second time I cheated death in Rio occurred at Copacabana Beach. I lingered on the less populated south end of the beach one afternoon where I overheard a group of young men speaking English. I walked over and said hello. They welcomed me with a cold *cerveja* and I learned they were from Thunder Bay. I gave them some recommendations about local jazz and bossa nova nightclubs and we eventually parted.

The next day I returned and went for a swim. The waves were crashing in a way that invited body surfing — a skill I'd mastered as a teenager at Bondi Beach, Australia. I swam out and repeatedly tried and failed to catch promising waves. Nothing worked. I began to tire and decided to swim back to shore. To my alarm I discovered I was far out at sea! People became colored specks in the distance as a deadly rip current carried me further and further into deep ocean.

Wave after wave tossed me around like a rag in a washing machine. My strength waned and I began choking on seawater. Efforts to swim at 90 degrees to the rip achieved nothing. I was drowning.

My thoughts turned to how sad it would be, simply vanishing without a trace in the ocean. My family in Canada might not even learn my fate.

As I was about to slip beneath the waves forever I glimpsed a hopeful sight. Two tiny heads popped into view, just visible above the turbulent sea. In time they became larger and I could see arms ploughing through the water.

Lifeguards! I thought. Two men were coming out to rescue me!

It took every last ounce of my energy to tread water until they reached me. When they did, they each removed a swim fin and affixed it to my feet; then the three of us locked arms and, with our combined power and the fins, made our way slowly back to the beach onto which they dragged my sputtering, vomiting corpse.

Someone poured water from a bottle over my face. As I gradually regained some composure, my eyes focused on male figures standing above me. It was the men from Thunder Bay! In time they revealed they just happened to be driving along *Avenida Atlantica* when they saw someone struggling in the ocean. Realizing the person was drowning, they'd driven down to the beach, flagged down the lifeguards, then drove back and sent them into the water to rescue me.

Simply put, had I not befriended those men and had they not driven by and caught sight of me out in the ocean, I would have drowned.

My third death dodge was even more dramatic. I was joined for the final two weeks of what was supposed to be an eight-week trip by my friend Matthew. After a couple of days Matthew and I were robbed violently at gunpoint in my apartment by two blonde-haired people — a man and a woman — for whom I opened the door on the mistaken assumption they were a Canadian couple I was expecting that afternoon, whom I'd never met.

As I opened the door, the man produced a large revolver and pointed it at my forehead, pressing me back into the apartment.

We're in trouble! I exclaimed to Matthew, who was oblivious in the living room, though not for long.

The couple moved fast in tying us up. The woman cackled and appeared to be high on drugs. The man was coolness distilled. They ripped my bed linens into strips to improvise rope-like restraints. First they tied my wrists together behind my back, then they tied my ankles together. Last they tied my ankles to my wrists. I was face down on the floor, trussed up and utterly helpless. A cloth was used to gag my mouth.

Matthew was tied up in the same way, though the couple never got around to tying his feet.

The seriousness of our situation was underscored by my having arrived back to my sixth floor apartment the week prior to find the hallway swarming with police. The young German tourist who rented the apartment across from me had been tied up in precisely this way and tossed from the balcony to his death.

They're going to kill us Matthew, I whispered. *If you're going to make a move, you need to do it now.*

Matthew's face was turned toward the wall and I don't think he quite appreciated the terminal nature of our predicament. He didn't fight back, and I can't blame him. It would have taken the skills of a ninja to jump up and overpower the man with the gun.

While we lay there immobilized the couple gathered all our cash, camera equipment, passports and other valuables in a bag. After some time — and quite a few episodes of my being kicked in the face and pistol-whipped — the thieves cleaned us out.

Why are they hanging around? I wondered.

To my everlasting terror the answer presented itself in the form of the woman grabbing a pillowcase and wrapping it around the muzzle of the gun. She stood over me and planted her feet on either side of my head.

As she lowered the gun I realized the pillowcase was to keep the gun clean of blood and brains as she shot my head off. She began to squeeze the trigger when, at just that moment, the doorbell rang.

And rang and rang and rang...

Whoever was on the other side of the door, out in the hall, was persistent. The male robber quietly approached the door and looked through the peephole.

Gringos! he whispered to his accomplice.

Eventually the door ringers departed. The robbers feared they'd gone to find help, and perhaps for that reason changed their minds about killing us. They left, locking the door behind them.

It was fortunate the thieves never tied up Matthew's feet, as this gave him some mobility. He deliberately knocked a drinking glass to the floor, then held a shard between his teeth and used it to saw the cloth bindings from my wrists. Once my hands were free it was quick work for me to untie the two of us. Disturbed but euphoric from having narrowly escaped execution, we eventually made it out of the apartment and on to the airport and home after obtaining emergency funds from the US and Canadian consulates.

For months and years afterward I contemplated the strangeness of my escaping death three times during that Brazil trip, most especially the last incident and the peculiar timing of that doorbell ringing.

Was that really just a coincidence? I wondered. *Are there such things as guardian angels? Or did some psychic force or emissary from another dimension send real flesh and blood people to press that button?*

Such questions haunted me, eventually spurring my interest in Buddhism and other spiritual modalities by the time I moved to California a few years later.

To this day I entertain the possibility that I did, in fact, die that day on the apartment floor in Rio de Janeiro, with my subsequent years of life flourishing in some parallel quantum dimension — a slice of the multiverse in which I survive the attack.

* * *

A few months passed before I felt ready for another session with ayahuasca. Again I signed on for Friday and Saturday back-to-back sessions at a rural retreat center, this time with facilitators who were new to me and quite young.

My previous fourth and fifth ceremonies had been led by Natasha and an assistant who normally works with mushrooms. This time, the ceremony would be hosted by Aarav — a young man who had apprenticed with Shipibo curanderos in Peru. He had a reputation in some circles for his innovative icaros, which incorporated modern beat box beats and were a very jazzy interpretation of the medicine song tradition. I wondered if his songs would change up my visions and experience.

He would be joined with a co-facilitator, a woman — Bolormaa — with whom I'd struck up a friendship after encountering her via some research into local ceremony providers. She was reputed to have the voice of an angel, which went nicely with her Pre-Raphaelite appearance. This ayahuascera had experienced hundreds of ayahuasca ceremonies and had studied with a *maestro curandero* in Peru.

These two facilitators were supported by two assistants. The first was Jim — a young man with less experience, who nevertheless was able to help in every aspect of ceremony and sang a number of his own icaros. He had experience in preparing the plant medicine and was well versed in the botanical sciences, which came in handy on this particular weekend, in light of what was to unfold.

The other assistant was Bolormaa's partner — Tiger — a young man also following a shamanic path who, at that time, primarily offered musical support.

My main concern was not knowing the facilitators well. I wondered about their age and experience. Yet I had encountered the medicine before, and while I certainly could claim no *mastery* over the plant, it seemed we were entering in a deeper relationship. I felt I could manage whatever might come up.

For this occasion I upped my game and volunteered to pick up the male ayahuascero at the airport. Aarav was arriving from Hawaii, where he lived, and he'd somehow missed his scheduled flight. Was this an omen? His ride couldn't gather him at the new arrival time, so I offered.

I knew I'd recognize him on sight from his YouTube videos. Bolormaa had given me his passport name in case I had a problem locating him. (He normally went by the Hindi name he'd picked up in India.)

On arrival he was as striking an individual as I'd imagined, with long hair and a beard, decked out in authentic Shipibo-patterned handmade cotton clothing, of the sort I wore in ceremony. He wore the same canvas surf shoes I generally wear for such occasions.

As we wheeled his luggage through the airport I attempted to make small talk.

So, where are you from? I asked, thinking of which US town or state.

From the stars, he replied.

I chuckled, and then realized I wasn't going to get a further, more terrestrial answer.

Fair enough, I thought. *No more small talk...*

Aarav slept most of the way on the long drive to the other facilitator's house where he'd stay until the day of ceremony. There wasn't much conversation, so I relaxed into enjoying the celestial chanting CD I'd put on for my guest's enjoyment.

As we drove through the beautiful green farmland northwest of Toronto I realized that being an assistant to these folks, or any kind of guru type, can be a pretty thankless task. You'd best help because you want to help, not because you need any kind of praise.

My thoughts meandered to what it must have been like to be a groupie or a roadie back in the 1960s and 70s. For sure there would have been some great parties, but also days and days of boredom, with tedious work loading and unloading trucks and vans full of equipment, rolling up cables and wires, labeling them, waiting around... all for the big day and the arrival of the "star" or "stars." Then tearing it all down and loading up the vehicles again. And again.

Yet here I was, part of something... the revival of psychedelics in North America. As someone born in 1960, I'd hit my teenage years just when the best part of the counterculture had exhausted its sex-drugs-and-rock-and-roll trajectory. My adolescence felt like arriving at a party just as it's winding down with people passed out everywhere, empty bottles strewn around, evidence of sex lingering, with people starting to put on their coats to leave.

Now it was returning, with me young enough to participate, but old and wise enough to guard against the excesses. I daydreamed in the car of my own path entwined with cathartic forces passing through the bowels of civilization.

I dropped off my guest, had a short visit with Bolormaa and Tiger, then drove home to wait out the two days before ceremony.

At one point it seemed the ceremony wouldn't be held at all. Bolormaa called to inform me there was a complication. A pretty serious one, in fact.

The plant medicine hadn't shown up in time for the ceremony!

Someone in Vancouver was supposed to send it by courier to Ontario, but had instead (incredibly) put it on a Greyhound bus. While Greyhound operates a reliable delivery service, it wasn't nearly fast enough to get the bottles of plant medicine to Ontario in time for the first ceremony.

CEREMONY SIX

Despite there being no medicine, I set off for the location on the afternoon of the scheduled first ceremony.

In the late afternoon people began arriving and within about an hour roughly 20 would-be participants were present. Each person set up their mats and blankets, pillows and sleeping bags around the large room that we adapted for this purpose.

The facility was set in the middle of a large outdoor recreational area. The building was primarily an industrial kitchen on the south side, with a narrow cafeteria-style set up of tables and chairs and a lunch counter. On the north side there was a medium-size dining hall that became our ceremonial space.

I was joined for ceremony by a female friend of mine — Ruma — a yoga instructor married to an industrialist. She set her mat down beside mine. She was apprehensive about her first ayahuasca experience, and I reassured her things would likely go well due to her years of discipline and spiritual training. We'd had many long conversations about a wide range of esoteric subjects, including Sufi mysticism and the online talks of Terence McKenna.

If ever a person was spiritually prepared to work with plant medicines, it was her.

As usually happens, people sat around chatting and getting acquainted while we waited for the sun to go down and the ceremony to begin.

The lead facilitators and their assistants arrived at our makeshift ceremony space, and called for everyone to sit down, as they had some news to share.

They explained that the ayahuasca brew had not arrived, due to its being placed on the bus. It hadn't turned up in Toronto, as had been hoped.

Aarav said they had sufficient ayahuasca brew on hand to serve all participants present one decent-size cup each. The challenge was for anyone wanting a second cup later in the evening, as people commonly prefer. And of course, we were there for two evenings, so something had to be available for the Saturday ceremony.

In place of the usual imported brew, Bolormaa and Aarav had devised a substitute for the second serving. They said this would be perfectly adequate, but for the sake of integrity they were clear about what was being prepared. They offered a full cash refund to anyone who decided this was not acceptable.

The alternative on offer would substitute the usual chacruna with an extract of DMT-rich mimosa.

Assistant facilitator Jim was in the industrial kitchen beside us, cooking up some old ayahuasca vines he'd purchased years ago. Sections of the vines had been boiling away in large pots all afternoon.

The facilitators said that the effectiveness of this preparation remained unknown, but that it should work like regular ayahuasca.

I weighed the pros and cons of all this in my mind. I felt inclined to drink the brew. Ruma was a bit nervous.

Then the facilitators threw another curve ball, stating they would not themselves drink the medicine that they were offering us. They said that their relationship with the plant required them to only drink the brew made with chacruna leaves.

Aarav said he was so sensitive to the plant that just being in the presence of people drinking ayahuasca was enough to transport him to the other dimension. The two assistants offered that they *would* drink the new brew. That was reassuring. After some deliberation all the participants (including Ruma) agreed to accept the new plan.

I had brought along some (non-hallucinogenic) Amazon bark tea I'd purchased from a friend who lives in Lima, Peru.

The bark — which looked like pencil shavings (and smelled like them, too!) — was contained in paper pouches and labeled to reflect whether it was the variety most beneficial for men, or the one best for women. I was interested in it as a possible mild potentiator of the ayahuasca, and offered it to others.

I walked through the heavy door of the industrial kitchen and set about making some of these bark teas in two metal cauldrons. After each tea steeped in the hot water, I decanted it into one of two thermoses for later consumption.

I learned a great deal about how ayahuasca is prepared, watching Jim standing like a druid over the bubbling cauldron. He was an amusing guy, too, and we joked around a lot. Things got a bit more serious when Bolormaa and Aarav entered the room and spoke incantations over the brew to infuse it with their special intention.

All of this was done guardedly. The facility managers would have taken a dim view of what we were actually doing in there as opposed to our cover story, which was that we were holding a "yoga retreat."

At times (rather hilariously) some of the baseball-cap-wearing groundskeepers or site managers would walk into the building and even enter the kitchen. Jim and I played it cool and told them we were brewing medicinal teas. It helped that I had information sheets on hand, explaining the health benefits of my bark teas.

These yoga people love their exotic teas, I recall blurting out, in the understatement of the year.

As the sun set, everyone sat or lay down on their mats in the designated space and Aarav initiated the ceremony.

First the facilitators "sealed the container" with a series of prayers. These were spoken in Spanish, but I made out that they were invocations to various totem animals.

The facilitators agreed to take turns throughout the evening checking on the vat of ayahuasca vines boiling in the kitchen near us. Participants took turns walking to the front of the room and sitting before Aarav, who determined the strength of the medicine each of us would drink, which was served by Jim.

Jim would pour the pure ayahuasca brew, then add a carefully-measured shot of mimosa extract (which was transparent and colorless).

Earlier in the day I'd spoken with Aarav and mentioned that I wanted only a small cup that night. So I was surprised when he instead ordered Jim to pour a large cup.

Mui fuerte! he said in Spanish to Jim who was kneeling to his right.

I was disturbed by this and whispered to Jim I'd prefer a small cup. Instead I received a cup filled to the brim, some of which I spilled on my ceremonial clothing when I drank it down.

This violation of my request set me on edge, and concern about it came into my thoughts throughout the night. Yet I coached myself, thinking almost out loud that this might be the plant's intention, working through the shamans.

I rallied myself: Was it not within my mental power to manage my expectations? Was I going to let this detail distract me from a beautiful and rewarding experience?

I later learned from Jim that he'd given me only about a medium dose of the mimosa extract, thereby achieving a compromise. Sure, the cup was full, but the psychoactive component was more measured.

Of course, I didn't know this at the time and lay on my mattress feeling trepidation. To distract myself I walked to the bathroom to wash the light stain of medicine out of my clothing. I then returned and lay down.

As expected, the medicine hit after about 40 minutes. When it came on, the effects were very powerful. I went into deep visions for several hours and at times lost any sense of my egoic self during the psychedelic roller coaster ride.

I experienced all the intense visual phenomena of previous ayahuasca journeys: the red/green geometric pattern; the three-dimensional objects and rapidly morphing creatures made up of brilliantly colored lines; and the more robust carnival and dreamlike landscapes filled with nightmarish or beautiful elements, including everything from laughing Mexican Day of the Dead skulls to light-filled energy beings.

The colors were beautiful beyond belief. My field notes record,

...neon pinks, blues, greens, yellows and electric orange...

There were landscapes, animals, lots of jeweled snakes, and also snakes with a more sinister aspect. They were vaguely reminiscent of paintings by Amaringo, but much more vibrant and complex, with everything moving.

As I usually do, I spent the first 45 minutes or so complaining to myself that it was all too overwhelming, and promising myself to never drink ayahuasca again! Over and over I told myself, *I must never forget I can't handle this! This is the message I must not forget! To never come here and do this! Never again!*

It seems funny now, but at the time I was serious.

After a while I sat up straight and concentrated on exercising my power to toggle between light and dark visions, getting comfortable in difficult circumstances.

Many times the visions would get dark. Fascinating animals appeared, and glittering luminous snakes that had the look I associated with ayahuasca's ability to be either benevolent or sinister.

God, but it was overwhelming! And such *hard work*!

Time and again I allowed the visions to get dark and then used my willpower to pull them up into the light. I felt like the pilot of a small plane deliberately going into a dive, then pulling out of it and heading above the clouds into sunlight and blue sky. And then I found myself deliberately flying into the darkest clouds, with thunder and lightning... disoriented, spinning... only to pull up and out again and fly my consciousness into the light.

I felt I was experiencing the Divine, and she was teaching me to navigate my way in hyperspace. I had a great opportunity to workshop this ability over what seemed like an hour or two. Whenever I felt I'd plummet completely over the other side and that my body would dissolve, I focused on my breathing and remained grounded.

Over the course of the evening the medicine came on in waves, each one a bit more manageable than the last. The gaps seemed to last about 20 minutes, during which time I could walk to the bathroom or take a drink from my water bottle. My field notes record,

At one point I realized it was impossible for me to reach out my hand and pick up the water bottle that was right beside me on the floor!

And Praise Sweet Baby Jesus! I didn't feel any nausea with this medicine! People were purging around me, but I had no seasick feeling.

No doubt my graduation into a nausea-free experience was aided by the fact that Jim had used both a cloth strainer and then cheese cloth to filter the brew. This removed small particles that, Jim explained later, contain tannins and other chemicals that upset the stomach.

The brew was much more liquid or watery than others I'd tried. I noted in my journal the next day that this is something other people who cook ayahuasca should consider. Innovation is possible with the chemistry of ayahuasca medicine and there's no reason for it to have an unnecessarily burdensome texture. Can we not innovate in this area, while respecting past traditions? I think so.

So it was fitting that not only was the medicine itself that night an innovative brew, but so were the icaros.

Aarav's medicine songs had a powerful and unique effect on me. He sang beatbox rhythms and strange intonations, via which his voice mimicked a range of musical instruments. It was odd and very modern and, surprisingly, it *worked!* Not only did this modern version of the icaros not get in the way of my visions and journeying — they augmented the experience and took me in new directions.

Everything I saw had a jazziness, at times almost an Art Deco aspect. Though it may offend traditionalists, I loved it!

When the second psychedelic wave came on, it was still powerful, but not as overwhelming as before. The evening transitioned into visions of a heavenly nature. Enormous emotions of joy and ecstatic reverie filled me up; I experienced the One-ness with Brahma consciousness that I imagine saints feel, and remained in a state of deep bliss for extended periods of time.

The visions were increasingly accompanied by specific teachings. As I'd intuited before the event, I was invited to a seat at ayahuasca's *adult table.* I was asked to step into my power. Ayahuasca manifested at times as a grandmotherly voice. I was given tough lessons from a kind, deeply ancient spirit.

Grandma reminded me how much I'd forgotten from my previous ceremonies. It was heartbreaking to realize how little I could actually recall the morning after a night on the medicine. I was shown exotic visions over and over and reminded that I'd forgotten them, and the medicine told me I'd likely forget them again.

Remembering is extremely important, I was told, and I was responsible for implementing the lessons later in the three-dimensional dimension.

At one point I became a king walking on the grasslands of Africa. When I lay on my inflatable mat I was reclining on a royal couch. I was treated to a sense of divine entitlement — really our collective entitlement — to be kings and queens in this beautiful realm, the natural kingdom of our world.

Nothing about this was egoic: The crown on my head was made of cardboard and it was clear we must remain humble. At one point I placed my vomit bucket upside down on my head and wore it as a clownish crown.

After this lesson I was given the lion's spirit, but told not to go looking for it in visions: I am the lion and must assume the lion's strength and confidence. I'm a male lion surrounded by lionesses who care for me, and for whom I must care.

The feeling of being a Zulu-like warrior king wearing a lion skin robe lasted a long time, and I modulated it with looking through the lion's eyes.

I interpreted this later as the medicine restoring my masculine confidence, which had taken a serious hit when I grew up with a father and stepfather whose sarcastic comments and unkind remarks about my appearance sometimes undermined my self-confidence. Ironically, they had also role-modeled masculinity and success and physical accomplishment, some of which also permeated my being. The Zulu warrior lesson, which was as realistic as something conjured up on the Star Trek holodeck, restored a shine to my being, putting a masculine spring in my step.

The music jibed beautifully with this and I stood up and danced for an extended period, standing and swaying in a special energy. I was allowed to feel my power as an elder — initiated in the shamanic culture. I was given lessons in humility but also in assuming my place in the world with confidence, supporting the world's shamans in their work with the medicine and other modalities.

Again I was reminded of the Story of the Mother. It was made clear to me that I have more work to do honoring all the mothers I know, helping them and writing to them about my love for them. I have many letters to write that can be a blessing to these beautiful beings.

Ayahuasca holds a feminine energy; it seems her lessons often revolve around maternal issues, which have application for both men and women.

Hers are also usually lessons in contrasts. She is dualistic. She shows both light and dark, male and female, good and evil, heavenly and hellish. As in life, with ayahuasca one has to work very hard to penetrate this dualism to find the still point in the turning wheel, the place of pure love and non-duality.

At times I suffered and cried, especially at the icaros sung by the female lead facilitator. Bolormaa had the most beautiful voice. I laughed and I wept, and felt a deep empathic humanity. I mourned the suffering in this world and the way things are out of balance. I was shown that Mother Earth would restore balance: it's just up to us whether that rebalancing is gentle (if we mend our destructive ways) or violent (if we don't).

I was shown again how the realm of ordinary consciousness is an illusion, but I was scolded about having described it sometimes as *just* an illusion.

Don't you realize? La Madre asked. *This is my greatest creation and I want you to live fully in it!*

As illusions go, it's pretty good, don't you think?

It was as though I'd seen behind the stage of all creation, and was being directed to return and protect it (as the living work of art that it is). I experienced deep appreciation and gratitude. I was invited to celebrate this dimension and to live, to thrive and to dance ecstatically. As the night wore on, this became an insight of great clarity to me.

I was given instruction about the path forward. I was to serve the cause of environmental protection even more fully than I had in the past. Again and again I was told to restore the Earth to balance.

Then something strange was communicated to me, something almost too odd for words. The nearest I can get is to say we're already living in the *Escaton* — the transcendental object at the end of time to which Terence McKenna often referred.

It's already here: we're living on it. *It's this planet!*

And it's not in the future. *It's right now!*

In a way that reminded me of the concept of Yugas, I was taught there is no past and future — only the eternal now. The time of the Kali Yuga (an age of darkness and ignorance) can be right now, or a Satya Yuga (a golden age). We can move things in either direction personally and as a broader society.

You and I can ourselves live in a Satya Yuga, even when surrounded by others manifesting a Kali Yuga (or any of the other four Yugas).

I was told to used my gifts as a writer to bring more people to shamanic plants to be healed, and again I was also told I must *remember*!

My field notes record a telepathic voice saying,

> The more you can remember, the less often you need to sit in ceremony.

Going forward, I understood, would be less about seeing what's in the other dimensions and more about *taking care of this one*.

I received teachings in how those other dimensions create and affect the ordinary three-dimensional one. Some of this reminded me of Don Juan's teachings in the Carlos Castaneda books. They were colorful immersive teachings, rich in imagery. I was shown things, not simply told.

I must pay greater attention to all living things, I surmised: learn about and appreciate them. Even spiders are mothers — manifestations of the universal consciousness. It occurred to me that more trips to the jungle lay in store. *I need to go deeper and see more!*

A portion of the night immersed me in dream-like experiences of reincarnation. These teachings would torment me for months afterwards, challenging my fundamental western understanding of reality.

Each of us has lived thousands of lives, and as different creatures. We're sent into this dimension like avatars, and made to forget. Until we return. *After we die.*

Is it possible, I wondered?

Again and again the answer was *Yes!* And every time I doubted, the teaching would resume, and I was shown a hundred if not a thousand of my previous incarnations.

A consciousness shift is underway in regard to that, I was told — one that's necessary to restore balance. I intuited the plant communicating to me that the Internet itself is one means via which the Gaian Oversoul is spreading her vines around the Earth. It came to me like a whisper of milk flowing from a stone colossus just behind my ear.

As the night modulated in and out of different moods, Aarav sang without accompaniment and at other times banged on a hand drum or played the guitar. His music was rhythmic and passionate. He'd sing with a reggae twist, or hip-hop, or dub step.

Bolormaa and Tiger sang also and sometimes moved about the room performing water ceremonies, painting our faces and hands with a feather dipped in cool water.

At other times the assistants blew *mapacho* tobacco smoke on our different chakras, or played different instruments like sparkling chimes or gongs up close to our ears or chests, triggering otherworldly sensations and visions.

I stayed up the whole night and never napped. It was a long ceremony, but I happily endured, and pushed healing energy from my heart out into the room. I was not just a recipient of the energy in the space, but a co-creator.

At times that otherwise mundane room felt like a ship built with glowing alien technology, taking us on a journey of transformation through space.

Eventually, in the early hours, the ceremony wound down and formally concluded with thanks offered to the animal spirits and the cardinal directions.

A few candles were lit and those of us who could manage sat around communally in the center of the room and snacked on finger foods laid out on a small carpet. We spoke and laughed and reminisced about the journey we'd just shared.

The room vibrated with an amazing energy.

I hugged Ruma, who shared some details about her awesome night, which had gone very well. She'd had a gentle but profound experience, feeling the plant medicine move through her body cell by cell, resetting everything.

Eventually I fell asleep on my mat just as the first yellow glow of sunrise crept into the room.

The most merciful thing in the world, I think, is the inability of the human mind to correlate all its contents. We live on a placid island of ignorance in the midst of black seas of infinity, and it was not meant that we should voyage far. The sciences, each straining in its own direction, have hitherto harmed us little; but some day the piecing together of dissociated knowledge will open up such terrifying vistas of reality, and our frightful position therein, that we shall either go mad from the revelation or flee from the light into the peace and safety of a new dark age.

— H.P. LOVECRAFT, *The Call of Cthulhu*

I woke up later in the morning after ceremony, now Saturday, after a few hours of fairly solid sleep. My body was a bit sore from its not resting in its usual bed.

My first concern was to find my other drug of choice: coffee. I wanted to mainline it...

I entered the cafeteria area of the mostly-empty building and approached the restaurant-style counter near the big doors to the industrial kitchen. A large stainless steel commercial coffee maker, about a meter high, sat on the counter, along with some jars of coffee grounds. I didn't know how to operate the machine, but in time one of the facility site managers showed up and taught me how to use the equipment.

In the midst of his instructions, I became vaguely self-conscious about my attire, as I was still wearing the Shipibo-patterned cotton ceremonial clothing from the night before. The contrast was stark between my costume and that of the site manager, who wore a conventional shirt and trousers and ubiquitous baseball cap.

As I waited for the coffee to percolate, my self-consciousness grew as a series of stout middle-aged men wandered into the cafeteria from outside, each holding an empty coffee mug. They wore canvas pants or denim jeans, red-and-black lumberjack shirts, boots and John Deere baseball caps. It turned out they were attending a half-day workshop on the grounds nearby on "How to Repair and Maintain Chainsaws."

You can't make this shit up, I thought to myself.

The contrast between my purpose and theirs at the facility was pretty hilarious. I'd come a long way from the thatched maloka in Peru, that was for sure.

A bearded member of that party chatted with me while we waited.

You folks here for a yoga workshop, I hear, he said.

Yep, I answered.

Those the clothes you wear for yoga? he asked.

Uh huh, I said.

Finally the red light came on the machine and we each filled our cups with the elixir of the gods.

It was a sunny day, but I whiled away most of my time indoors, writing notes about the previous night's ceremony and brewing up more pots of the male and female versions of my Amazon bark tea in the big kitchen.

I enjoyed hanging out with Jim while he brewed more ayahuasca vines in a large pot. We'd have no shortage of the psychotropic liquid that night.

I'd hoped to sleep in a special Hennessy tent hammock I'd brought with me (that has its own sewn-in cover). You climb in and out of it through folds underneath, like re-entering the womb. But instead I spent the rest of my time interacting with participants from the night before, and new ones as they arrived.

The facilitators spent most of their time in some rented cabins on the property, recovering from their drawn-out night of intense effort.

I enjoyed long conversations on the grass, but eventually felt the need to move my body. I went for a walk on the property and eventually found a small river that one of the site supervisors had told me about. I saw a turtle sunning itself on a rock.

Sign of the shaman, I thought.

I stood for a while under an enormous ancient oak tree that reminded me of the one in the Disney animated film *Pocahontas*. She provided a great towering home to ants and birds and — looking up into her massive branches — I wondered how long she'd stood majestically in that field.

How many winters have you endured? I asked. *And how many burning hot summers?*

This is the beautiful hologram in which we live, she seemed to answer, echoing the previous night's lessons.

By the time evening arrived and the shadows of the trees lengthened like great fingers, some of the participants from the previous night had left (including Ruma). New ones had arrived.

It all felt somehow *perfect*.

CEREMONY SEVEN

The ceremony got underway in the same manner as the previous night, with smudging, prayers and invocations. I missed having Ruma beside me, and prepared for another possibly long night.

When asked to approach the front, I again asked the facilitators for a small cup. Thankfully this time, I thought, Aarav will instruct Jim to pour only a small…

Oh heck! I thought. *He just told him to pour another large cup!*

It was full almost to the brim! I drank it with trepidation and returned to my mattress.

I lay there speculating that the facilitators had discussed this beforehand and decided to trick me. I'd told both Aarav and Jim earlier in the day that this evening I *really* wanted a *small dose*. Had they conspired to say I'd get a small cup and then give me a large one? I doubted this, but wasn't sure.

After a while I decided it didn't matter, and that my own mind was messing with me. (The next day I learned Jim had again served me a large cup, but only a medium portion of the mimosa extract.)

After the medicine came on, the first hour or so was intense and filled with extraordinary visions. Again I didn't suffer nausea, perhaps due to the filtering of the brew. For this I was deeply thankful.

The visions were overwhelming at times, but I sat up and focused on my breath. I worked at moving my visions up into the light rather than downward into the dark.

After the first peak of the medicine, the remainder of the evening played out gently, just as I'd hoped.

This is a common pattern with ayahuasca — an intense night followed by a more gentle one (and sometimes the reverse). For this reason many facilitators prefer that novices sign up for at least two sessions, held close together. This way they get to experience at least two sides of the plant teacher.

Vision after vision came in waves. It's not hyperbole to say they were the most beautiful I'd ever experienced. *Ineffability* was their defining characteristic. I received many teachings about my path forward and about integration. There were times when it seemed I received a lesson every minute!

Time and space don't apply here, I thought.

Some lessons were general, but some were highly specific. The themes, which I wrote in my field notes the next day, included that

> I am to be in the service of the Grandmother medicine (and to be of service generally), to build community, and to bring people to the plant teachers.

Many messages were dark and powerful. I can report them like rational thoughts, but there's no language to convey their emotional power.

The Earth is in crisis, I was shown over and over, and like a sheriff fighting a gang of outlaws, the plant medicine deputized me to join in the battle to save the town.

My mind flew like an eagle over vast forests and mysterious landscapes. I could see empty cities blowing with detritus, and journey through eons of human and animal consciousness.

Some kind of non-corporeal consciousness kept telling me, *You can become a shaman or not — the job title doesn't matter.* It just wanted me to waste no time. To take action.

At times I sat and looked through the dark at the facilitators and assistants. I realized they're not larger-than-life super-humans — just people like me, doing their best to be of service, and making sacrifices. Their reward was some sort of ecstatic joy — a joy I was now feeling.

Somehow I received clarity about websites that could be home for my writing. My role was not only to tell my own story, but to assist others in sharing theirs.

I'd set my intention for this night as "To integrate the first night's lessons," and this is precisely what happened.

Forgetting is the price you pay for coming here, the medicine voice said, many times. The grandmother seemed to laugh at me, though in a kind way.

Oh grandmother!

The evening was punctuated with many interruptions, but these were not unwelcome. Everything happened as part of a perfection. Certain people had difficult nights: nights of rebirth in the fire of resurrection.

Bolormaa and Aarav went to work on certain individuals who were suffering, singing songs to the whole group but sitting directly in front of these people. At other times they performed specific rituals only on them.

A great sense of community permeated the room and I looked for ways to help. In the middle of the ceremony I checked on someone who'd wandered out of the building and appeared to have gotten lost.

We were like a tribe in a longhouse, connected intimately, purging near one another, experiencing all manner of joys and sorrows.

I was haunted by the sense of what we've lost, not living communally, staying apart as individuals and nuclear families in separate dwellings. A large baronial estate home seemed like the definition of hell: prisons for the rich.

We all live in prisons now, I thought. *Our cages are just different sizes.*

The facilitators had a wide range of techniques and healing strategies: splashing a light spray of flower water or blowing tobacco smoke. Bolormaa treated me to a water ceremony, stroking different parts of my face with a large wet feather, stimulating a new vision:

I lay on my back looking up from inside a forest with very tall trees. It was a bit like an Emily Carr painting. In the sky there was a yellowish-white light, but it wasn't the Sun exactly. It began to swirl and swirl upon itself as it drew my consciousness up inside it. My mind entered the swirling light fully.

From that point onward my visions were supremely radiant and divine.

I recall feeling someone working on me while I was deep in the medicine, having a wave of visions. Tobacco smoke was being blown on me.

I opened my eyes partially and sensed it was Jim. With a simple gesture he signaled to me to sit back and not talk.

He worked on my limbs and different energy centers and I overheard him blessing me and saying almost under his breath that I would henceforth never again be afraid of spiders. (And this has been the case.)

After perhaps two or three hours Aarav sat at the front of the room and — speaking plainly — thanked the other facilitators and especially Bolormaa for their exhausting work, for stretching themselves to care for people who had challenging nights.

Aarav conducted a ceremony to close the container. It was then safe to leave the building. He invited us to step outside and take in the night sky, which glowed an eerie red on the horizon, with the Milky Way dazzling directly above us through faint clouds.

Everyone was up and about in the cool night air, and we spoke with one another and congratulated ourselves on our work so far that night.

In the distance, way out in a field, Bolormaa sang to the cosmos while playing a harp. It was a sight I'll never forget, straight from a Pre-Raphaelite painting.

After we returned inside the building and our sacred circle, Bolormaa sang some beautiful icaros and also some modern songs. We were all coming down from the medicine. Only a couple of people had taken up the offer to drink a second cup.

Aarav, it appeared, had slipped off to bed and didn't return. At first this distressed me a bit, but I later realized this person had a brilliance for changing up the pace, keeping people a little off-balance and encouraging them to stretch themselves.

Perhaps because he wasn't there, some of us felt more comfortable offering the group our own songs, which Bolormaa invited us to do.

I sang a melancholy chant I'd somehow channeled that very afternoon while walking near the river. I called it "Sadful Joy, Joyful Sadness." It appeared to move people and it certainly moved me: I felt a swelling from inside and it seemed like I was calling upon the spirits of the ancestors. The medicine, even its trace effects, allowed me to exceed my normal limitations.

Later I sang a dirge I'd written and performed a few months prior at a graveside ceremony that my family organized to consecrate my stepfather's headstone. It had been powerful singing it then, and it was powerful singing it now.

Filled with an uncanny and indescribable joy, I somehow I drifted off to sleep. I thought to put on my eye mask, which allowed me to remain asleep when the sun rose soon afterwards.

In the morning sharing circle I was urged to continue on my path and develop more songs. I said to the group that each person should use the medicine to heal themselves, but to not stop there.

Look beyond yourself, I said. *Build community and help others. Once you're a healed person you have the power to heal others.*

It felt more like the medicine was speaking through me than that I was talking.

I felt immense nostalgia as we packed up our sleeping bags, our blankets, our mats and our other paraphernalia. It was like a circus had come to town, put up its big tent, and now was being dismantled.

I left the meeting place filled with joy about the blessed road ahead.

Do not be dismayed by the brokenness of the world.

All things break. And all things can be mended.

Not with time, as they say, but with intention.

So go. Love intentionally, extravagantly, unconditionally.

The broken world waits in darkness for the light that is you.

— L.R. KNOST

In the weeks and months that followed my sixth and seventh ceremonies — held over a single summer weekend in 2014 — things began to shift again for me, in almost every imaginable way.

The routine duties of my day job in the trade magazine industry became a hair shirt. I was well-paid and worked from home. It was a job to die for, really. And yet...

In my mind I was a wandering sadhu, naked and covered in ash.

The shift went beyond mere dissatisfaction with work. My thinking cycled on the concept of superstitions, to which

I became present more and more every day. My assumptions about culture and even the nature of reality were a like a corpse stuffed in a barrel in the basement, slowly dissolving in acid. I was afraid to go down there, in case anything was left. Or lest it came back to life. My questioning of superstitions dated back to the mid-1980s, when I lived for a year in Santa Monica, near the famous pier.

A neighbor named Fionnuala (Irish, of course), who was recovering from cocaine addiction, used to come over for drinks with my landlady at the small house in which I rented a room.. My landlady confided once that Fionnuala shared her bed with her two adult sons. One learns of such strange things in Los Angeles.

Despite her predilections, I owe a debt to Fionnuala for taking me to a popular New Age bookstore called The Bodhi Tree, where I loaded up on books and tapes about spirituality and higher consciousness. One was a recorded speech by Werner Erhard, the founder of EST (now known as the Landmark Forum).

I'll never forget Erhard repeating over and over again, *a superstition is only a superstition when it's not a superstition*. This opaque phrase was a succinct way of saying we're conditioned with beliefs that silently control our behavior; they do this most successfully when they're just below the level of conscious awareness.

Real superstitions, in other words, have power because we don't think of them as superstitions. In contrast, encounters with black cats or walking under ladders have no real power over us.

Erhard was suggesting we're literally *slaves to our minds*.

While I lived in Santa Monica, and on the month-long drive back to Toronto, Canada, I listened to this speech many times and contemplated its mysterious message. *What are the superstitions?* I wondered.

Money came to mind right away. And the concept of *time*. Then there was *work*. And reporting to a *boss*. A person selling their time in exchange for money under the supervision of a boss was deeply embedded in superstitions, I surmised, unless that person broke free mentally somehow.

We have superstitions about *love*, and some of our most profound superstitions, of course, concern *death*. And the nature of *being*.

Does death really exist? And what is life? Are we living in a simulation?

Are we Brahma's dream?

After experiencing ayahuasca, I intuitively began living in a more Zen-like way. What had been an intellectual system of ideas yielded to authentic felt experience. I was not yet fully up to speed with the concept of shamanism, but as the superstitions lost their power over me, my Buddhism became a way of being rather than an ideology.

In a way that was liberating, my life became *meaningless*. When I wasn't preoccupied with *anything*, I opened up to *everything*.

People commented that I'd changed. Something was different about me. I dressed differently. My priorities shifted.

One day I set up an altar in my living room in which I installed shamanic items. One item was (and remains) a bust of the god Hermes that I sculpted in high school, copied from the statue by Praxiteles in the British Museum. I'd lugged it around with me all my life through different houses and apartments.

Hermes (Mercury to the Romans) is a shamanic deity. As psycho-pomp, he's the only god able to descend into Hades and reemerge unscathed. His duties include guiding the souls of the departed to the edge of the River Styx, where the bargeman transports them to the afterlife.

Hermes is a symbol of transformation, magic and resurrection, who likely evolved from the falcon-headed Egyptian god Horus. As a child he'd fashioned an instrument from the shell of a turtle and invented music. With his winged feet, he's the messenger of the gods and also a patron of travelers. Across the ancient Mediterranean, travelers would wear a charm fashioned into the head of this god, and tie their transport animals to posts with the head of the deity carved on top, known as *herms*.

The decolonizing of my mind continued that had begun at the Nihue Rao Spiritual Center. My political philosophy evolved. Bored and restless, in the fall of 2014 I finally gave my notice, agreeing to work until the last day of December of that year.

When I left the job I was able to finally make a deep dive into all the material I'd been salivating to read or watch for years.

Throughout 2014 I wrote freelance articles for a range of websites and magazines. Chief among these was Reset Me — founded by former CNN reporter Amber Lyon, whose life had also been changed by drinking ayahuasca in Peru. I wrote a few pieces for the consciousness shift website Reality Sandwich and maintained a regular blog on the Pulse Tours website. I wrote a travel-style article about the Peru trip for *Get Lost* — an Australian travel magazine.

I began to garner a small reputation as a commentator on psychedelic and shamanic topics.

Heeding the teacher plant's admonitions, I joined the board of directors of a small philanthropy called the Amazon Rainforest Conservancy (ARC), founded by Ontario resident Jana Bell. ARC's mission is to fundraise in industrialized countries and to secure long-term contracts to maintain Brazil nut concessions on pristine lands in the Amazon to protect them from exploitation by loggers, ranchers and wildcat gold miners. The organization had already purchased hundreds of hectares in the Madre de Dios region of Peru near a fairly lawless area heavily contaminated by the mercury used to distill gold from river silt.

In 2014 I helped edit and publish my friend Michael Sanders' book *Ayahuasca: An Executive's Enlightenment*. That book richly reports the 10-day Peru trip Sanders and I shared with the other travellers over New Year's Eve, 2013-2014. I rank Sanders' first literary effort alongside Malcom Lowry's *Ultramarine* as a classic in its celebration of introspection in a setting of exuberant travel.

All this activity constituted the early beginnings of what I came to realize would be years of integration work.

* * *

In the summer of 2014 I again felt ayahuasca's siren call, which I heeded by accepting an invitation to attend another weekend of back-to-back Friday and Saturday ceremonies, again with Bolormaa and Tiger. (Aarav would not be present, as he'd returned to Hawaii.)

CEREMONY EIGHT

This ayahuasca ceremony — my eighth — was special from the start. Indeed, it ended up being unusual even by the crazy standards of my previous journeys in the tryptamine space. It included my first experience of a physical substance brought forth from the spiritual realm.

I'm not a follower of astrology, yet I confess the heavens were shining prophetically on our event. The day — a Saturday — was the Hindu day of *Guru Purnima* — a festival dedicated to spiritual and academic teachers that falls on the day of the full moon (purnima) in the month of Ashadh (June–July). I'd attended a lecture about Guru Purnima the night before, so was up on this. Coincidentally, news on the car radio mentioned this night would include a rare "super moon."

The drive took a couple of hours, as the venue was in cottage country about 90 minutes northeast of Toronto, while I lived at the time about 90 minutes northwest of the city.

I arrived with Debra — a woman I'd been dating for a number months. We were both pleased to discover near-perfection in the setting: our ceremony would take place in an off-grid retreat center powered by wind and solar energy, built and maintained by an older man with a bushy grey beard who reminded me of the hippie comic *The Fabulous Furry Freak Brothers*.

A wind turbine whirred high and loud above us as we unpacked the car and carried our pillows, blankets and other gear into the cool adobe-finished interior of the two-storey main building. The owner showed us around, pointing out how to use the energy-efficient appliances and shower.

In the large upstairs yoga studio a few people who'd stayed over from the Friday night ceremony slept on small mattresses prepositioned along the walls.

I recognized a few souls from previous events and said hello. So as not to awaken the others, conversations were conducted in whispers.

I arranged my pillows and other items on a mattress I selected in one corner. These included the small colorful medicine bag I bought in Peru, in which I kept must-need items. I set my purge bucket on the floor beside my mattress.

In time the other participants arrived, and I greeted each with a hug. (There were no handshakes in this crowd.) Our group numbered about a dozen and included my girlfriend plus another three close female friends of mine, which may have boosted my energy that evening. There was my yoga teacher friend Ruma, who was accompanied by her dark-haired daughter Akna. And then there was Sade — a female friend I'd dated briefly who'd followed my writing and adventures and was keen to try the plant medicine.

Debra and I tried going for a walk on the main road, but the area was heavily forested with mosquitoes out in force. We turned back hastily.

We then joined a group of participants sitting in a mish-mash of salvaged patio chairs around a smoky fire in an outdoor pit near the main building. The smoke seemed to keep the bugs at bay. While we waited for the sun to set and ceremony to begin we engaged in stimulating conversation that was interrupted often as we moved our chairs to escape the smoke, which changed direction frequently with the breeze.

In time Bolormaa and Tiger appeared from another building where they'd been resting. Debra and I headed inside and lay down on our mats. I noticed an older man playing with a baby. His younger girl-friend — the child's mother — arrived: an attractive woman with long flowing black hair.

The facilitators eventually took their place at the front among an altar-like configuration of musical instruments, crystals, feathers and various bottled unguents.

As I lay on my mat, my thoughts included a mild sense of irritation about the girlfriend I'd brought to the event. Couples often sit on opposite sides of the room during ayahuasca ceremonies, so their energies and other involvements don't interfere with what are supposed to be individual journeys. Couples can sometimes lie beside one another, which can be all right. But I sensed Debra had joined this ceremony for the wrong reasons — to be with me, and not to work on her own issues.

It was like I was going skydiving or bungee jumping, and she was along for the ride, not because it was really important to her to drink ayahuasca.

As night fell and the room darkened, the ceremony began.

Bolormaa invited us to stand with her, raise our hands, and turn through each of the cardinal directions as she offered a prayer for protection to the spirit animals such as jaguar and eagle.

My heart pounded furiously and I began to sweat in anticipation as we sat down and shared our intentions for the night. These ranged from simply "healing" to more complicated requests. I set my intention as, "To heal my family," by which I primarily meant my mother, sister, stepbrother and myself. All were mourning the passing of my stepfather two years prior and wrestling with vestigial patterns of family dysfunction.

Bolormaa poured the brown ayahuasca medicine in careful measures from a large plastic bottle. Going around the room counterclockwise, the participants approached the makeshift altar one by one and knelt before her. Most said a small prayer before tilting their heads back and downing the liquid.

I eased my tensions a little by turning to each of my female friends and wishing them a good night and a good ceremony. I told them I was Dracula and they were my brides and we all had a laugh.

The medicine was another factor in the power of the events that were about to transpire. This was no ordinary batch brewed casually by indifferent assistants in some Amazon lodge or — God forbid — purchased on the streets of Iquitos. The medicine had been handcrafted by the facilitator herself and a team of adepts in an exotic land. They'd rhythmically pounded the *Banisteriopsis Caapi* vines in unison while under the influence of the brew itself. A prayer had been made for each chacruna leaf as it was washed by hand.

Such details are important to adepts of shamanism. I once mentioned to a shaman friend that I planned to buy a hand drum for journeying, which triggered advice about the importance of making the drum myself, harvesting the wood from a special tree, finding the right animal skin, holding a ritual while washing it, and so on.

And here we had just about everything right, in shamanic terms: the setting in an off-grid house under a juicy moon, the talented facilitator and her assistant, an exotic brew, and a gathering that included four friends. I'd come prepared, having maintained a strict ayahuasca diet in the weeks leading up to ceremony.

After drinking a brimming cupful of medicine I lay down on my mattress and stretched out my back, in (accurate) anticipation of sitting up for much of the night.

I lay still for about an hour, waiting for the medicine to come on. Nothing happened. It was only the second time I'd felt no effect from the first cup of ayahuasca brew. Just as I was thinking this, the facilitator (who'd been wandering the room singing and interacting lightly with people) invited us to drink again.

I hesitated, not wanting to drink a second cup in case the first cup's effects came on late, but Bolormaa reassured me not to worry.

Guardedly trusting her, I drank a second time, the liquid tasting (as always) like coffee left on the burner overnight.

In no time the second cup hit me with force and I slipped into visionary hyperspace, overwhelmed with intensely colored geometric patterns beyond the capabilities of any Persian carpet weaver.

Crystalline visions filled much of the night — shimmering realms that only a Coleridge or Keats could describe. A kaleidoscope unfolded of radiant spirit emissaries, turreted cascading temples and mercurial skies so beautiful I wept.

As always, amid the psychedelic visions there were lessons.

During the first hour or so I received a stern teaching from the medicine about how it's her job, not mine, to decide whose experience of consensus reality is to be interrupted. The universal consciousness created this dimension and prefers that creatures embedded in it experience it as real, without people like myself calling attention to its being any kind of illusion. Or at least, not by cajoling them to consume psychotropic plants.

Just as I wouldn't interrupt someone engrossed in a video game and say, *Hey, it's just a game!* I'm to leave people in their immersion, unless they're actively seeking to awaken.

Like a drill sergeant, the medicine asked me over and over again, *Whose job is it to pull people out of the illusion?* with me answering, *You, eternal mother!* and again, *Whose job is it to pull people out of the illusion?* with me answering, *You, Mother Ayahuasca!*

The medicine backed off after the first peak and I sat up. I positioned a fabric yoga chair to support my back and settled in to listen attentively to the sacred icaros sung beautifully by Bolormaa, with Tiger's guitar accompaniment. Sometimes she played a Jews harp, or struck symbols or other odd noisemakers.

I watched her dance from mattress to mattress, gesticulating in silhouette like some crazed Haida bird creature, at times channeling the ancestors in a high-pitched glossalalia. I really saw her shape-shift into this therianthrope and ever since have been quite clear about where the ancients got their inspiration for deities that are half human, half animal.

At certain points I felt Debra's eyes on me, which I found irksome. Just as I'd imagined, she was paying attention to me when she should have been concentrating on her own inner journey.

At one point, right when I was in the depths of a demanding but profound experience, she touched me lightly and asked if I was all right. I brushed her away, losing some of the visionary transmission during the exchange.

During all this I forgot about my intention: *to heal my family*.

Then I felt a shift in my stomach system: the two large cups of ayahuasca were working their way through my digestive tract. I used one short sober intermission to assess things.

Did I need to throw up? Was I about to have diarrhea? I couldn't tell for sure, so I decided to head downstairs to the bathroom, while I still could.

A telepathic voice told me, *Bring your purge bucket*.

As I stood up the medicine came on again. Still, I was able to find my feet and slowly walk barefoot across the wooden floor toward the dimly lit stairwell that led below.

I was near the top of the stairs when the inner voice said, *You'd better hold your container close to your face*.

Thereupon followed a series of truly volcanic heaves like I'd never experienced, even from the plant medicine. The cosmic retching came from the deepest core of my being and no superlatives can do justice to the sheer animal spasticity of it. It was loud and accompanied by horrid gurgling sounds similar to those of the lead curandero from my first three ayahuasca ceremonies in Peru.

I felt the eyes of the people in the room on me and a few offered sympathetic comments of the *Way to go!* variety.

Vomiting is common in ayahuasca ceremonies and people had been purging all evening. Knowing the healing that accompanies it, it's a sound I'd grown to like. I often prayed or saluted in the direction of people healing this way.

I knew that after this enormous purge my stomach would feel fantastic for the rest of the night. And the barfing — dramatic as it was — didn't hurt at all. I had a queer sensation I'd thrown up many issues that belonged to my family members.

Was it possible that I'd *taken one for the team*?

Had people who were not present in the room somehow been remotely healed through me? Or through the facilitator?

I made my way downstairs and wandered across the darkened main floor to the bathroom. My plan was to empty my purge bucket in the toilet, and wipe my face.

Everything looked normal and I wasn't hallucinating: plain old toilet, sink, faucet and walls. A small lamp sat on the vanity for illumination.

As I proceeded to the toilet another telepathic thought entered my mind.

Look inside the container.

I held the clear plastic jar directly under the lamp's bright light, perplexed.

It was not vomit! At least not in any conventional sense.

The container held a dark semi-transparent liquid with the texture of mucous. The color was the black-green of a night sky just before a tornado descends. Through the transparent sides of the container I detected fibrous dark cloud-like matter. Looking closely into the top, the surface formed a white phlegmatic foam that then retreated toward the container's circular inner sides. The center of the liquid depressed while the sides appeared elevated, and the surface began to pulse up and down like the skin of a drum.

Remembering a scene in the movie *Alien,* I wondered if something was about to jump out at me, and pulled back my head. At that moment dark bubbles foamed their way to the surface. I looked uneasily until I made sense of what I was seeing.

Eyes!

What I first mistook for dark bubbles were hundreds of black eyes looking out at me from inside the container. My skin turned gooseflesh. These weren't human eyes with whites and irises: they were insect eyes, like those of spiders, all glossy and black.

And they were pissed off! They were *furious*!

In an instant I sensed I was looking at spirit entities — dark forces that had attached themselves to my family and lived with us parasitically for generations, even centuries. They stared out at me, angry beyond description at having been found, and now they were trapped in a kind of inescapable shamanic phlegm.

It was hypnotic looking at the sea of eyes. I asked myself if they could just be bubbles, but over and over again the answer came, *No, those are eyes!* I felt their intelligence looking out at me, and their venomous rage.

I began to fall under their spell and thought for a moment about putting the lid back on the container and somehow preserving the liquid. I was like a character from *Lord of the Rings*, spellbound and trembling when holding the ring of power.

Then, without further hesitation, I poured the liquid in the toilet and flushed. At first it wouldn't go down but after two solid flushes it was gone, and along with it (I believed) the source of much suffering over the years of my family.

I can imagine the skepticism an account like this will trigger in anyone uninitiated in shamanic experience. I'm actually as skeptical as anyone and doubted the event myself, except I was there and remember its impact.

Feeling both frightened and liberated, I returned upstairs and rejoined the ceremony, where I felt safe.

The ceremony lasted many more hours. I recall a night of extraordinary beauty, of visions and information downloads that followed one another in rapid succession. I was treated to viewing the world as a spider sees it, running across endless amounts of web in iridescent color. This went on for a very long time.

I became a snake and spent some of the night curled up, breathing as if through my skin. I experienced the sheer intensity with which these beings live!

Unlike us, who spend much of our lives working indoors, unaware of the weather or sitting stultified in front of television sets or computer screens, these creatures are fully exposed to the elements and engage in the daily life-or-death battles of predator and prey.

No animal in nature dies of old age, I recalled my stepfather once saying.

The medicine suggested I befriend a spider.

Let it live in your house. Learn from it.

The final hours of the night were a kind of reward time. Everything was sweet and gentle. Ayahuasca asked me why I never asked her about life in other parts of the galaxy.

I created all that, too, she said. *Would you like to see how things are on other planets?*

Yes, I answered, and was treated to a guided tour of beings in other star systems and galaxies. I recall tall thin gauze-like creatures vaguely reminiscent of jellyfish, except they floated in the atmosphere, and long conical stretched-out creatures that reached from near the ground into the sky. I saw many different vistas and life forms as bizarre as anything conceived by science fiction illustrators.

In the final hour or so before the ceremony ended I felt great happiness but also an intense nostalgia. Half intoxicated and half sober, I was in the liminal space of grey mists haunted by psychopomps and the tricksters who can cheat death. The visionary landscapes in their rainbow beauty began to fade, and I felt sorrow over everything I was about to forget.

This is the shaman's burden, I thought languidly. *To see and know too much.*

To be aware that this world is an illusion. God's dream. And to be laughed at or scorned for one's strange claims.

Did we think we could enter the realm of the dead and not pay this price?

11

Death belongs to the realm of faith. You're right to believe that you will die. It sustains you. If you didn't believe it, could you bear the life you have? If we couldn't totally rely on the certainty that it will end, how could you bear all this?

— Jacques Lacan

The fall of 2014 was a challenging time for me. In September I had only four more months remaining working for the magazine conglomerate to which my business partners and I had sold the business in 1990. My 25-year career in trade magazine journalism was about to end.

I'd ended my relationship with Debra and I felt listless living in the gated development in Collingwood.

My interior world was falling part. Perhaps it's more accurate to say it was being *rearranged*.

The colonizer's disease of *wetiko* had left me. This Anishinaabe term expresses the narcissism of European settlers, whose imperiousness toward other human beings and disregard for the natural environment was viewed as an illness by the indigenous people of North America.

The ongoing decolonization of my mind put me further and further offside of the materialist culture in which I found myself embedded. I was like an Aztec who no longer believed in the Sun god. I couldn't relate to my culture and its superstitions.

The accumulation of possessions felt emptier to me than ever before and I had no desire to hold power over other people or attain any kind of social status. I started giving things away and tossing out anything in my apartment I didn't really need.

It was challenging to simply be *me* at times, because people continually interacted with me as my old self. I came to view Guy Crittenden as a role, as in a stage play. Initially, this felt very inauthentic, like I was an imposter.

Eventually, however, I came to appreciate Guy Crittenden as a wonderful part, which I could play lightly to move through the world. It helped me to think in terms of *The Matrix* film trilogy; whenever I left my apartment to run errands, socialize or engage in work-related business, I reminded myself I was entering the world of the machines and Agent Smith.

Guy Crittenden was a very fluid being now. He could participate in mundane human interactions, but he danced, both literally and figuratively. He was in the society, but not entirely of it.

During most nights the paranormal activity continued, which I realized was shamanic experience. I'd wake up to strange audio hallucinations or lie in bed in the early hours bathed in white light, which shifted and glowed like the Northern Lights. I rode magic carpets of sacred geometry that arose spontaneously, and occasionally remote-viewed whole vistas that opened up before me.

My spirit animal visited regularly, and I tried to cultivate the relationship and understand its strange meaning. I welcomed it when it visited, expressing gratitude and love as best I could.

In time I felt the call to get this animal — the sacred anaconda — tattooed on my left arm and hand. This was partly in homage to the very first time I heard of ayahuasca. Many years before, I'd flown home from a business trip in England and had sat beside a hippy chick from the BC Interior and her young baby. The woman was a dead ringer for

Liv Tyler, who was in the news at the time because the first of Peter Jackson's *Lord of the Rings* films had come out.

On the long flight she told me about the medicine and traveling into the jungle to drink it with shamans. I was struck by a tattoo of a snake that wound its way from her shoulder to her hand, executed in a stylized Gaelic pattern. The mouth of the serpent extended around the arc between her index finger and thumb.

Ayahuasca's first signpost, when I was immersed in family and corporate life...

Another phenomenon presented itself also that autumn. I'd been on a paddling trip with my brother and some friends in Northern Ontario. We were a couple of days into the trip, and I was in the stern of a rented canoe crossing a large lake. The sun was out and the water was fairly calm. I closed my eyes for short periods as we paddled, my arms executing the familiar J-Stroke on autopilot.

I noticed that whenever I closed my eyes an exotic pattern appeared against the red of my closed eyelids, illuminated by the Sun.

The pattern was dark, but not quite black, and circular.

How to describe it? It was similar to a silhouette cut with scissors from dark construction paper — the kind one can buy at carnivals. The complicated pattern inside each circle was made up of very stylized human beings, animals and geometric forms. They reminded me of Mayan glyphs or temple illustrations from ancient Egypt or Sumer.

I blinked, wondering at these faint but wonderful visions, which changed often.

I struggled to keep the canoe on a straight path. My companion in the bow didn't notice I was paddling with my eyes closed much of the time.

We came to a floating dock attached to a large island, where we ate a packed sandwich lunch. I sat away from the group, often lying on my stomach on the wooden dock in order to gaze undistracted at the silhouette glyphs.

The canoe trip was also notable for another kind of psychedelic experience my brother and I enjoyed together, which was the consumption of psilocybin mushrooms on a beautiful pine-covered promontory one sunny day, after the rest of our group departed for home.

I unpacked the mushrooms, which were in powder form inside capsules. We decided to eat three each to start, and then eat one more capsule every 20 minutes or so, up to a maximum of six, to dose ourselves properly.

I offered a protection prayer to the cardinal directions and their totem animals, and we downed our first batch of capsules with water from a flask.

The medicine came on slowly for both of us, and our experiences seemed to move in tandem. The psilocybin's first effect was hyper-acuity. The edges of leaves and tree branches became more clearly delineated than usual. Time began to slow down

After strolling around a little, we spent the next hour or two at our campsite before heading across a small inlet in the canoe and walking in the forest there.

We rested beside a creek across which an enormous tree trunk lay: black, cool and covered with moss. I shimmied to its center and lay on my back. I stared up into the tree branches for a long time, inspecting everything with what I later called "God vision."

My ordinary perception shifted: instead of only being able to focus on one thing at a time, I took in the whole scene around me — every detail — all at once. This allowed me to see the Fibonacci sequence in the repeating lengths of branches and twigs. The forest canopy revealed itself as a vast wooden cathedral ceiling.

* * *

In mid-Autumn I felt called to drink the ayahuasca medicine again, and accepted an invitation from a local facilitator with whom I'd not sat before: Don Carlos. He was a friend of Bolormaa and had been one of her most important mentors in the ways of the medicine.

Bolormaa referred to him as her *maestro,* as she'd apprenticed with him for some time, after first apprenticing with a curandero in Peru.

I was eager to meet this person and invited him for a drink in a restaurant a few weeks before ceremony. He was an unassuming man, and almost avuncular in comparison to the larger-than-life fantasy character conjured up by my imagination, thinking of a *maestro.*

At this meeting I learned more about the plant medicine and how this particular facilitator had studied it. He'd started holding local ceremonies about 15 years prior, long before ayahuasca was popular in North America.

I learned that the upcoming ceremony was to be held at the same off-grid facility northeast of Toronto as my last one, which pleased me. I looked forward to experiencing Don Carlos's style and energy. It would be my ninth journey with the plant medicine.

CEREMONY NINE

My ninth ayahuasca ceremony was a blessed experience that adhered to the parameters I'd set out earlier that day, which mostly pertained to my desire to have a gentle experience.

I was getting tired of my powerful reactions to the medicine, profound though they were. All had included hours of strong visions and harrowing lessons from the universal consciousness.

Was it possible to have a rewarding experience without having my ass kicked so badly? I wondered. I hoped to obtain the "Goldilocks" dose — neither too big nor small.

I arrived at the facility with my friend Ruma and we unpacked the car quite quickly. It was good to meet the bearded owner again, and re-familiarize myself with the pleasant adobe-style decor, the white walls, the tiled floor, and the large yoga studio on the second floor that would serve as our ceremonial space.

Other participants trickled in, roughly half male and half female. The gathering ultimately included 17 people, so it was a fairly large group.

Most were experienced ayahuasca drinkers, many having sat over the years with the older facilitator. There were some tattooed and hip-looking people in this crowd; it looked like there were no novices at all. This boosted my sense this would be a good evening with few distractions.

As the sun set and the room grew dark, Don Carlos sat on his mat beside a small low table that was set up as an altar, covered with various shamanic objects. One was a small statue of the Virgin Mary

— the first time I'd seen a Christian icon at one of these events. (I later learned Don Carlos had done some work with the Santo Daime church and had incorporated some of its concepts and energies into his ceremonies.)

Don Carlos was flanked by female assistants, one of whom had colorful full-sleeve tattoos on her arms with ayahuasca themes. Very cool.

These women and some other people in the room turned out to be gifted musicians, and their participation contributed to the sound and healing throughout the night.

Don Carlos reviewed the rules and protocols and we took turns one at a time sharing our intentions. I stated that I simply wanted a gentle night and to reconnect with what I'd come to call, simply, *the Divine.*

The medicine was served at about 9:00 pm. Don Carlos told us this medicine included not only the usual ayahuasca vine but also a special variety of chacruna called the White Queen, thought to be especially potent in triggering visual experiences.

Because the group was large we went up two at a time.

In accordance with a conversation I'd had with Don Carlos earlier in the evening, he poured me only three-quarters of the small cup. I planned to ease into the experience, and only drink a second smaller cup later, if needed.

I was a seasoned drinker now, and wasn't going to be bullied by anyone into drinking one ounce more than I wanted. Sitting with this mature facilitator was emblematic of this, and he had a great attitude. As one finds with the best ayahuasceros, there was no ego involved in his actions. He was simply there to serve the medicine and hold space for the group.

I said a small prayer, drank and returned to my mat, noticing that this particular brew tasted closer to the sweet flavor of prune juice and a bit less like the burned coffee flavor with which I was most familiar.

I lay down on my mat and waited for the effects to come on while Ruma went up for her cup. After what felt like about 40 minutes, people around me started showing signs of being under the medicine's spell. Don Carlos sang icaros and walked around the room with a rattle, working on people.

A while later some people moaned gently, and from time to time someone purged, though not violently. At this time I felt nothing. No effects at all. *Nada.* I sat up at the end of my mat, legs crossed — stone cold sober — for about another 30 minutes.

At just this point — about 90 minutes after the first cup — I'm normally offered, and usually accept, a second cup of the medicine. Yet (thankfully) a second cup wasn't offered until much later in the night. I was about to learn something valuable.

Just as I sat there thinking the medicine wasn't doing anything, it began to come on, slowly. Within a few minutes I was deep inside an immersive experience, with beautiful patterns, creatures and landscapes whirring around me. The medicine crept up on me like a cat.

It frightens me to think how overwhelming it all would have been, had I drunk a second cup just before then. I later made a note to not drink another cup until after first giving the initial one a really long chance to take effect. I wondered if I'd "double dosed" myself in some previous ceremonies.

I accepted a second serving much later in the ceremony and, since I was still journeying, only drank a quarter of a cup, just to extend the experience.

I love the White Queen! I thought. *What a beautiful night this is!*

The overtly psychoactive portion of the night lasted until about 2:30 in the morning. During this time I experienced several waves of psychedelic effects, and also participated quite a bit in the music and singing, playing a small hand drum I'd brought during some of the more rhythmic icaros.

Toward the end of the night several of us got into a purely percussive drum session that had a great groove to it. People told me later they enjoyed listening to it.

This became a new thing for me, that I would seek in future ceremonies: the chance to participate in the music, rather than being just a silent retail customer — at least, near the end of the ceremony, when my favorite facilitators open up the floor to audience participation. (This was something Ricardo Amaringo had also encouraged near the end of ceremonies at Nihue Rao.)

The visions and journeys on that special night were too many to enumerate, but they adhered to certain themes.

One was animal, insect, human or plant forms of various kinds, that morphed constantly into different things. They were usually made up of hundreds of thin vibrating energy lines, comprised of vivid neon colors that strobed between intense orange and yellow, pink, mauve, blue and so on. These forms pulsated with life and consciousness.

The Gaian Oversoul showed herself to me like this in all her beauty, in thousands of different ways. At times the creatures and landscapes morphed into a mosaic pattern, as though every surface was created from tiny reflective pieces of highly-polished stone or ceramic glass. Often the colors softened into earth tones, without the neon quality.

My intention of being in the presence of the Divine was answered, and my field notes from the following day refer to this as being *lifted into the light:*

> Colored objects would at times manifest into a most intense white or slightly tinted light. Another light was a reddish glow — as if from a log fire — that often emanated from the left side of my field of vision.

The room was completely dark and my eyes were closed, yet I saw this light often. Sometimes I opened my eyes to check if someone had lit a candle, but they had not: the red light was purely in the psychedelic space.

Sometimes I'd see a more naturalistic scene, which often accompanied a lesson. These visions were like lucid dreams. In one I realized I was extremely old (in my eighties or nineties). The skin on my hands was wrinkled and I was aware that my face was heavily lined and creased. This was a preview of my own old age. I was allowed to feel what it would be like.

Interestingly, it was clear I would still be sitting in ceremony. The medicine showed me *this is my path*, and that I will be acquainted with teacher plants for the rest of my life.

Ayahuasca flows in my veins, I thought.

Because the medicine wasn't overwhelming (though it was powerful) I sensed I'd remember more of my visions afterward, and this turned out to be the case.

A static painting wouldn't capture the flow of the ever-changing images, which moved like lava. It would have to be an animation, a film. But the more impossible task, the thing that a film could never capture, was the sense of *presence* that informed the visions — a profound awareness. When I later encountered the writings and talks of physicist Tom Campbell, author of *My Big TOE (Theory of Everything)*, I associated this awareness with the background consciousness that he describes as not belonging to this reality frame. Just as the person holding the controller of a video game provides the consciousness of his or her avatar from outside the game itself, the universal awareness that experiences our thoughts and sensations emanates from beyond our physical reality, which is why we'll never really find it in atoms here.

I recall learning there is no inner world and outer world: they're expressions of one thing, in a Yin-Yang relationship. Ayahuasca is like a hack of reality, allowing us to experience the big mind holding the controller in a dimension beyond ours.

In the end, I had exactly the experience I'd hoped for: a powerful yet gentle night with many visions, but no unbearable first hour. I was very grateful for this, and felt renewed enthusiasm to participate in ayahuasca ceremony.

After Don Carlos closed the ceremony at about 2:30 a.m. a few of us went outside and sat by a roaring campfire under the stars. It was one of the clearest skies I'd ever seen, with the Milky Way incredibly brilliant and many constellations crystal clear.

I then returned to my mat and slept until about 9:00 a.m., after which time I joined the others for breakfast. A conversation was held at 10:00 in which we shared our accounts of the previous night.

As often happens, people's stories were all over the map.

I knew one woman had had a difficult night, because she'd lain in the middle of the room crying in a cathartic way. It was more like howling, actually, than crying; she'd been comforted by several other participants and Don Carlos, who had worked on her.

Several people had experienced very dark and disorienting nights in which they thought they were going to die, and couldn't figure out up from down or even where the floor was. One woman had endured feelings of great hatred, as though she was purging an inner demonic force.

So much for my theory that experienced drinkers had it easier than newbies. I was thankful for the beautiful night I'd had.

As I packed the car in the morning and prepared to leave, Ruma pointed out the beautiful blue sky we were enjoying. I mentioned that those lovely stars we'd seen the night before, while sitting around the campfire, were still there — we just don't see them because of the sunlight.

Ayahuasca is like that, I said. *She shows us the divine cosmos that's normally hidden from our view, as we live in this consensus reality.*

I began to rediscover the beauty and magic in this dimension that I usually take for granted.

I became a child again, amazed at the wonder of it all.

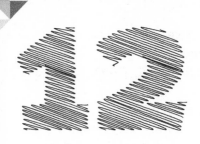

Where love rules, there is no will to power;
and where power predominates, there love is
lacking. The one is the shadow of the other.

— CARL JUNG, *The Psychology of the Unconscious*,
1943

About a month later I accepted an invitation to drink ayahuasca again.

I arrived at the location for my tenth ayahuasca ceremony
feeling a bit agitated. The thought of the intensity ahead
quickened my pulse. Akna was with me — the daughter
of my yoga teacher friend Ruma; she helped bring in our
sleeping bags, pillows and other gear from the car. I thought
it would be interesting sitting with her without her mother
present.

The ceremony was to be held in Bolormaa's house. I was
now friends with her and Tiger, with whom I had grown to
feel a special connection. I adored the beautiful music these
two made together: Bolormaa's singing voice was exquisite,
and the love of the two of them bathed the entire space.

In shamanic terms, I felt Bolormaa was the radio tower on
the hilltop, transmitting the energy of the Divine down to

me, the little transceiver in the valley. Something special augmented my ceremonies with her that I could never quite put my finger on.

Was it the music? Was it the light-filled medicine? Or was it some spiritual connection beyond my understanding?

It was likely a combination of all these things.

Bolormaa gave me a big hug when I stepped into the foyer and remarked that I seemed nervous.

Damn, she was so intuitive!

After a while I calmed down, especially after I brewed some Amazon bark tea on the stove and poured it into a thermos for later in the night. All would be well.

That morning I'd eaten only a small bowl of granola for breakfast and some bagels for lunch. These things filled me up but wouldn't swish around in my stomach during the ceremony (a strategy I recommend).

I drank only water for the rest of the day, and hot water (to simulate tea) in the evening. The hot Amazonian tea in the thermos was reserved for the early hours of the morning, when the ayahuasca medicine wore off.

As I set up my thin Therm-o-Rest camping mattress and pillows in the ceremonial space, I was pleased at the arrival of another female acquaintance with whom I'd sat in ceremony before, with Don Carlos. I ended up sitting for the night between this woman and Akna.

Space was tight in Bolormaa's living room, but not dangerously so. I socialized with the other participants, who were 10 in total, including the facilitators. As night fell I went downstairs and changed into my white Shipibo ceremonial clothing.

CEREMONY 10

Tiger directed Akna and me to a set of animal prophecy cards and invited us each to pull one.

I pulled the Turtle card and read the explanation. Turtle's meaning is extensive, and includes its being a symbol of the ancient Earth. An amphibious animal that lives between two worlds (water and land), the Turtle is a symbol of the shaman. Hermes — the Greek shaman deity

— had made the first musical instrument from the shell of a turtle. Turtle also represents grounding.

Though I put it out of my mind, much of the night fit perfectly with this card.

By about 9:00 p.m. everyone was settled in the ceremonial room. Several of the participants had never drunk ayahuasca before; some had only drunk once. When things were about to start I went around the room wishing them well for the journey ahead.

As things got underway Tiger turned off the overhead lights and the dark space was lit by only a single candle. Bolormaa passed around hand-rolled *mapacho* cigarettes that people could use later to clear dark energy, and we each took turns briefly describing our intention for the night.

As usual, people's stated intentions varied widely. As was now my pattern, my intention was simply to be *in the presence of the Divine*.

I wasn't coming to the medicine anymore for personal healing, but instead to connect to Spirit and reaffirm my commitment to service. It amused me a bit to watch newcomers focus exclusively on their closely personal problems, which seemed so enormous to them. Few had the insight, yet, that they are God in disguise. Over a number of ceremonies I'd observed some participants mature into deeper layers of selflessness and wisdom as they further penetrated The Mystery. I thought it a shame that some people drank only once or twice and never went deeper.

I sat on my mat reflecting on the impression I must have made, along with my fellow travelers, back in Peru during the ceremonies presided over by Ricardo Amaringo. It embarrassed me to think how ego-ridden our bunch of North Americans must have seemed to him, nattering on about our various First World neuroses (though he extended nothing but compassion).

Knowing newbies were present, I offered advice that if people find themselves in a very dark experience, it's sometimes a good idea to sit up and not lie down, which can exacerbate the feeling of being overwhelmed. I also passed along a tip that Amaringo had shared with my group in Peru: If you see a frightening apparition with which you don't wish to engage, simply imagine throwing a green net over it and send it up and away with a rope! Dismiss it!

I'd found this works very well.

As I might have guessed, after giving this "wise old man" advice, I then spent most of the night myself lying down and only sat up occasionally in the latter part of the ceremony. (Ayahuasca loves to humble me this way.)

Each of us was invited to drink our cup. Bolormaa and Tiger had sampled the ayahuasca before ceremony and told us this was the best medicine they'd ever encountered. I found myself in agreement by the end of the night.

What followed was a night in which I spent almost all of my time in the presence of the Divine, but in ways that were surprising and not at all like my previous ninth ceremony.

This night I had the usual fantastic visuals — as amazing as anything I'd experienced— but most importantly it was a night of crystal clear *teachings*.

It was also a night of *remembering*. I'd been frustrated with not being able to remember my visions in detail. But this night ayahuasca gave me lessons (over and over) in how to *remember*.

The night's themes initially recapped teachings from previous ceremonies.

You only need to come here when you forget! the medicine reminded me telepathically. *Remember that the real miracle is the dimension you normally live in.*

The more you can find the Divine in what you think of as the ordinary world, the less often you need to come back here.

I found myself imagining legions of angels lined up in columns, like paratroopers up in heaven, awaiting their chance to jump into incarnation.

My field notes remind me that all of this got off to a slow start. I drank only one cup of medicine during the night, rejecting the offer of a second. It took about an hour for me to cross into the tryptamine space. The first psychedelic wave came on slowly.

For a while I thought nothing was going to happen and I even played with the idea of escaping the experience and just lying there all night. (Many previous journeys had been so difficult.) But the medicine voice told me: *You will not get off so easily…*

Remember, it said, *when you said in the car you have the rest of your life to get a good night's sleep? You will work hard tonight!*

And that was true. The steady build eventually got me as far into hyperspace as I'd ever been. I tried sitting up and lying down, but the medicine voice laughed at me.

There is no escape!

Thankfully, the visual display was stunning, and I felt no nausea. I flew my consciousness through the usual panoply of complex geometric patterns, which shifted from being fairly flat into very three-dimensional.

I ended up standing in a vast, almost infinite room, larger than any cathedral or mosque, in which the walls and other architectural features were made of gold and silver. But this was not functional architecture. Instead, the walls and pillars and other shapes melted like hot wax, constantly changing. They morphed into various animals and insects — some very recognizable (a moth, for instance, with complex antennae, or a lizard) — and others I couldn't decide on before they became something else.

My notes recall my seeing a vast wall looming above me, extending into infinity:

> A shimmering pattern of snakes appeared, slithering down this wall. They weren't naturalistic: all of them were spaced exactly the same distance from one another, wriggling down the wall. They were perfectly shaped in their heads and bodies, and made of molten metal, like mercury poured from an immense thermometer.
>
> Instead of bearing scales, their skin was polished and smooth, with perfectly beveled edges, as you'd expect to see on a piece of cabinetry. In place of eyes, the snakes had jewels that reflected shards of light everywhere, like diamonds or other precious stones. Their bodies were inlaid with bevel-cut jewels. In addition to gold or silver, their metallic skins reflected hundreds of delicate rainbow colors.

The snakes weren't frightening; I knew them as heavenly messengers. Yet they did exude a kind of menace, a power, which suggested they were not something to mess with. I simply looked at them in awe.

Soon everything changed and other creatures appeared that were made up of hundreds of contoured lines.

Visions of this nature persisted for hours, especially when Bolormaa and Tiger sang their icaros: everything sped up, vibrated and whirled. My consciousness piloted through candy-colored thunderclouds and mountains sparkling with treasure. I realized this is the true nature of Aladdin's cave — a Persian psychedelic spirituality metaphor. And there was that magic carpet...

Often I sat up in the lotus position with hands in prayer, tears streaming down my face at the beauty. Sometimes I kissed my fingertips or fingered the crystal pendant that hung from a string around my neck.

My overall feeling was one of gratitude.

Gratitude, gratitude, gratitude.

Madre, aho! I'd whisper aloud.

At some point near the end of the first peak, the first distinct lesson came to me. It was another teaching on the importance of the mother. I encountered the Cosmic mother, the Earth Mother (Pachamama), and the mothers that exist throughout creation, from wolves to eagles, from fish to spiders, from lions to lemurs.

I was shown the mother's journey, her burden in childbearing, childbirth, raising her young to maturity, and (most poignantly) the pain of separation. This was not just some visual tableau. In fact, at this point in the night the visuals quieted down and I was guided through feelings.

Ultimately I simply felt *anguish.*

Then I felt a sense of dread, something building up inside.

What monster is approaching? I wondered.

Finally it broke.

I was made to feel the pain and heartbreak of *every woman who has ever loved me*, starting with my mother and then a series of girlfriends, my former wife, and lovers I have had.

I felt the way they loved me *from their perspective* and their *sorrow at parting.*

It was irrelevant whether there was a good reason to break up — I simply felt a woman's sadness — the deepest part of her sorrow in losing someone for whom she cares deeply.

At the very depth of this experience Akna, seated to my right, began to sing a song about lost love. It was achingly beautiful and transformed via the medicine into a true icaro.

I found myself sitting up at the end of my mat, and just when I thought of slinking back into a prone position, a telepathic voice spoke to me.

She's singing to you! it said. *Sit up and pay attention!*

I had to endure the sweet sorrow for a long time. Again I went to lie down and the voice said, *She's not going to stop singing until you understand the lesson!*

I knew right away that my friend also knew this somehow, so I focused. I realized the sorrow I was being made to feel was the grief of Debra — the woman with whom I'd recently broken up. I'd somehow excluded her from the list of past loves.

My logic in doing so carried no force in this courtroom of the heart. I had reasons for ending that relationship, but apparently I needed *to feel* how that person loved me. I then felt the kind of sadness that can drive a person to jump off a bridge or drink poison.

As soon as I *got the lesson*, my friend stopped singing. The medicine voice indicated that it was okay for me to lie down.

I was also given a very profound lesson about a mother's eyes: their compassionate gaze is one of the places where God resides. This was the first of several lessons in that regard: God's favorite hiding places.

If you need to find me, the goddess seemed to say, *look into that endless chain stretching back through all eternity of mother's eyes, starting with your own mother.*

I lay back and stared into the eyes of mothers. Human mothers. Animal mothers. Even insect mothers.

This lesson was followed by instructions in supporting all mothers and the role of the warrior. I was thankful for the presence of the two dark-haired women sitting on either side of me.

Another peak in the night was a lesson in *remembering*. This theme also applied to each of the lessons. Whereas I can often only glimpse ayahuasca lessons as though through a glass dimly afterwards, this night the medicine gave me strategies to retrieve lessons and apply them in my life.

One lesson I made an extra effort not to forget is difficult to explain. It was another of *God's favorite hiding places,* which turned out to be... the voice we hear constantly in our own heads.

Yes, the voice that's with us always that we think is *us,* is God also. It's not the only place God inhabits, but it's a favorite. Contrary to what we're told in meditation classes, the voice we try to quiet in meditation is also a place where God hides, laughing at our attempt to silence her.

After the first peak and a brief respite, the medicine came on again, strong.

Akna started to sing again. I was astonished at her range of expression as she was invited to sing several times. She channeled cosmic forces that night.

Bolormaa performed wonderfully and also took long breaks. We sat in silence at times for longer than usual. Bolormaa mentioned the next day that the person who prepared the medicine had said this ayahuasca was especially good for silence. I appreciated these gaps as a time to absorb the lessons and work on *remembering.*

The next lesson was an intensely visionary and immersive experience.

I sat in wonder in an especially beautiful landscape looking upward, trying to *go into the light.* Visions of more beautiful snakes and other reptiles appeared. I asked the medicine if things were about to turn dark.

What would you like it to be? she answered, implying I had a choice.

With trepidation I asked to go into the dark. I sensed a profound lesson awaited me there.

Quite quickly the beatific vision became realistic, as in a lucid dream, and I found myself floating in a bayou. I bobbed in shallow warm water and muddy reeds beneath a piercing blue sky and a beating sun. I felt like I was near New Orleans, and my mind made an interesting connection between this environment and blues music (for which I have a passion).

I spent the next hours floating around in these waters with various reptiles — mostly snakes, alligators, some frogs, and other creatures. These were realistic, with leathery hides and dark greenish brown skins and scales. They moved around me, sometimes entwining me and otherwise interacting.

No matter how much I thought about it, I didn't find any of these creatures frightening. The medicine voice almost *taunted* me to find any of it scary, yet I simply could not.

Then each of the creatures started toggling between its natural appearance and its metallic-jewel-encrusted spirit manifestation and the lesson became apparent: I'd always thought of the "dark" places — the realm of creepy-crawlies, centipedes, snakes and spiders — as sinister. However, they are every bit as much a manifestation of the Divine as the ethereal realm of light energy beings, rainbows and shimmering clouds.

This was a profound lesson. While there may be such a thing as "evil," the opposite of the Divine is not the dark that I associate with these creatures and their realms: they are simply different levels of life's beautiful complexity and novelty.

As I sobered up slowly and came fully back into my body, I realized I have a choice. Whenever I see something potentially frightening, I can re-imagine the medicine voice asking me, *What do you want it to be?* and turn it toward the Divine.

The following day I also answered a question: *What animal was I in that muddy bayou?* It was obvious: I'd been a turtle, which, with its hard shell, is inherently safe from the snakes and alligators around it. This was the card I'd pulled from the animal deck before. This had all been a great lesson in grounding.

The final major lesson emerged around the time the facilitators played some especially delightful music, in which I participated. This was in the last third of the ceremony, which went very late. I can't even guess what time.

Bolormaa came and sat directly in front of Akna, who was sitting crossed-legged at the end of her mat. The two of them looked like a pair of American Indian women, which suited the rhythmic song they began to sing faster and faster.

Something came over me and I felt the urge to stand up.

I was wobbly from the medicine and also because I was standing on my Therm-o-Rest. The medicine voice told me to anchor my right foot to the back and plant my left foot forward in a warrior pose, with my fists crossed in front of me, arms partially outstretched. I morphed into a First Nations warrior with long black hair.

I started to move in time with the rhythm of the song and, unable to really sing along, I clanked my wrist bracelets like a rattle or tambourine. Then, almost unconsciously, a drone started to emerge from deep in my chest and up my throat, and I began to chant, providing a deep rhythmic bass for the women's soprano singing.

Tiger joined in with a rattle and pretty soon the four of us really had something going. We built up the volume higher and the rhythm faster. We were inside a large teepee and I tapped into something very primal, my most essential humanity.

It all built to a crescendo and then the singing stopped, with the women collapsing into one another's arms.

My manifesting the warrior was powerful for me. It was interesting the next day when Tiger said he'd *seen my spirit* that night, which appeared to him as a bison or buffalo, with a large head and broad shoulders.

As the medicine gently subsided I lay down and processed a great many things. I eventually sipped some of the tea from my thermos, which was no longer hot but warm enough to soothe. I checked the feeling in my stomach and had no nausea or need to use the bathroom.

My mind slipped into a long meditation with visions of the mass extinctions taking place on our planet, especially of elephants, who are being killed for their ivory tusks at a rate of something like one every 15 minutes. Within a decade there will be no more elephants in the wild, and the same is true for many other animals.

As I thought about this the medicine voice again asked me, *What do you want it to be?*

I realized the same choice we have in the tryptamine space is one we have in the physical world. We can have seas devoid of whales and sharks and other species, and continents where no wild tigers, lions, or elephants roam, or we can live on a garden planet brimming with life. The power belongs to us to shape this fate.

The ceremony ended in the early hours before daybreak. I was amazed at the stamina of the facilitators.

After saying a prayer, Bolormaa lit a candle and Tiger brought hot tea from the kitchen along with some snacks. Most of us were still awake. A few people had drifted off but eventually roused themselves, joining in discussion about the amazing night we'd just shared.

We eventually went to sleep and reconvened again after daybreak for breakfast and a conversation in which we shared our experiences, passing a feather as each person took turns speaking.

Some people had had visions, while others had had more physical experiences of healing and cleansing.

Akna and I packed the car and headed home. On the drive I reflected on my long career.

My writing is my medicine bundle, was a thought that kept surfacing.

I can't imagine living in a world devoid of elephants, I said to Akna as I steered the car over a rolling hillside below large wind turbines that turned slowly in the breeze.

You need to work on solving that crisis, Akna said.

How do I want it to be? I thought to myself, over and over.

13

But then, perhaps, I have a feeling of mortality all the time. Because, if life excites you, its opposite, like a shadow, death, must excite you. Perhaps not excite you, but you are aware of it in the same way as you are aware of life, you're aware of it like the turn of a coin between life and death. And I'm very aware of that about people, and about myself, too, after all. I'm always surprised when I wake up in the morning.

— FRANCIS BACON, *Interviews*, with David Sylvester

The Maya fought not to kill their enemies but to capture them. Kings did not take their captives easily, but in aggressive hand-to-hand combat. A defeated ruler or lord was stripped of his finery, bound, and carried back to the victorious city to be tortured and sacrificed in public rituals. The prestige value a royal captive held for a king was high, and often a king would link the names of his important captives to his own throughout his life. Captives were symbols

of the prowess and potency of a ruler and his ability
to subjugate his enemies.

— *A Forest of Kings: The Untold Story of the Ancient
Maya*, Linda Schlele & David Freidel, page 143

Why are human beings so cruel to one another?

Is cruelty a uniquely human trait? Or has it risen up from the deep
reservoir of predation and suffering that flows back through animal
history, with tigers tearing apart deer, snakes swallowing mice, car-
nivorous dinosaurs chewing up herbivores, big fish eating little fish,
and even viruses infecting single cells?

In my life I've experienced all kinds of cruelty, but as I reflect on
my own family history, kindness and good vastly outweighed the
moments of family dysfunction that punctuated our collective narrative occasionally. My first ten ayahuasca ceremonies, and especially the
tenth itself, caused an upwelling in my heart that allowed me to both
face the awfulness of certain parts of that narrative and at the same
time forgive the actors and feel immense compassion for each family
member, especially my late father and stepfather, with whom I'd had
complicated relationships.

I can attest that a better relationship is possible with one's parents,
even after they've passed.

My mother Yvonne and father Max emigrated to Canada from
Australia in the late 1950s. They toured the world, as Aussies often
do, in their early twenties. My mom and dad looked like a couple of
movie stars back then. My favorite photo shows them wearing sunglasses, my mother's head covered with a jaunty scarf, sitting with a
friend along the cliffs over Acapulco on a sunny day.

They ended up in Toronto in 1958 and started a family soon after. I
was the first born, in 1960. My dad got a job at the *Toronto Telegram*,
and my mother worked taking care of a boarding house they operated
for a while, then as a secretary, before finally claiming a position as a
reporter, also at the *Tely*, as it was known.

Ours was a newspaper family, and my mom and dad advanced rapidly in their careers, through talent and hard work. It helped that they blended easily into the Toronto culture of the time, which was similar to that of Melbourne: white, protestant, and colonial. This was a culture of roast beef dinners on Sunday and reverence for all things British.

As an adult I learned that my parents had ended up in Toronto because it was the closest they could get to New York. My father's dream had been to launch a syndicated comic strip in New York and eventually live wherever he wanted, drawing his cartoon each morning before heading to the beach. He did, in fact, create a pretty good comic strip called *Ukluk* that lampooned modern society through a cast of Eskimo characters (Today we'd call them Inuit). He traveled to Manhattan to pitch it, but the bigwigs shot it down.

After that rejection, his cartoon dream faded and gradually Plan B became Plan A. My parents stayed in Toronto, and eventually divorced and remarried. When the *Tely* folded in 1970 my stepfather Peter Worthington cofounded the successful *Toronto Sun* newspaper, which eventually became a tabloid chain.

After a failed attempt to take a Montreal weekly newspaper daily, my father Max founded a small freelance editing and magazine graphic design company. This flourished until his multiple sclerosis came out of remission. After a slow decline from cane to scooter to wheelchair to hospital bed, he was dead by age 59.

Though we didn't grow up in a wealthy home, we may as well have. A press pass in those days was a kind of Gold Ticket to the front of every queue for every movie, special event, or amusement park ride. My sister Danielle and stepbrother Casey and I were like young royalty whisked around the city by my reporter mother to different events.

Max was a newspaperman molded in the Ernest Hemingway tradition. He was a chain smoker and heavy drinker, often to be found sitting with a beer in one hand and a cigarette in the other doing a crossword puzzle. His second wife, Carol, was less of a steady drinker and more of a binge drinker.

Alcohol abuse played a large role in busting up my birth parents' marriage. Though I have many happy memories, alcoholism tainted many of the times I spent afterwards with my father and stepmother.

My dad was a mean drunk who sometimes became verbally and even physically abusive. My stepmother was someone who hid her drinking problem, hiding empty bottles in drawers or under the bed. Eventually I became quite alienated from the two of them, though never completely.

If alcoholism impacted the Max-and-Carol family constellation, workaholism perhaps played a role in undermining my relationship with my stepfather. He was a wonderful father to me and my siblings when we were children, taking us on trips and going beyond the call of duty by teaching us to swim, letting us dive off his shoulders in the pool, playing tennis with me in the summer and shinny hockey in the winter. I have fond memories of him coming home from work most days and insisting on throwing the softball with me on the street in front of our house.

He was a man of action — physical activity relieved his stress and was a way he related to others outside of work. He also loved dogs; we grew up with several generations of Jack Russell terriers.

So it was very sad when we fell out as I entered my teenage years. I couldn't seem to get on the right side of him in those days. In some respects I relate: having co-owned a publishing business in my thirties, I'm aware of the pernicious effects of work and ownership-related stress. My stepdad became tightly wound up and it didn't take much to set him off. Something about me seemed to just bug him.

He was also a conservative columnist who felt his politics keenly and personally. As I came into my own as a young adult, I found myself offside of his views, which made for some tense dinner conversations.

In time a kind of magic circle developed with my stepdad, mother and sister on the inside, and my stepbrother and me on the outside, looking in — a dynamic that lasted for decades. Eventually the ugly arguments and tensions grew beyond the point where it was tenable for me to live under the same roof as my mother and stepfather. I moved into a rooming house downtown in my second last year of high school. I never returned, other than a brief stint in my final year of high school when I was cramming for exams. Then I was off to university.

In my mid-twenties, my readings in Buddhism offered a path via which I attained the best relationship I could with all the other members of my two family constellations. Things weren't perfect by any means, but I generally tried not to add fuel to the fire when conversations became tense.

Like precious photos recovered from a house fire, in the end some good things were salvaged. All was not lost.

When my father Max endured his long decline with multiple sclerosis, my capacity for compassion grew. I visited when I could and helped out sometimes with the various indignities that disease inflicts upon the human body. I wasn't holding any anger when he finally died. He was 59 and I was 35.

I was thankful to experience something of a rapprochement with my stepfather when he was in his eighties. When I'd come for dinner, Peter would offer to drive me home. I'd tell him I was happy to take public transit but he would insist. It wasn't hard to see he just wanted the chance to talk. Like many people of his war-tempered generation, he wasn't comfortable talking about his feelings, but in a roundabout way he communicated his appreciation of me, and his respect for my having pursued my dreams without seeking his (or anyone's) approval.

He'd ramble in the car about the old days, memories of my siblings and I when we were kids, advice on financial matters. There was no set script. When he died, things were good between us.

My ayahuasca journeys showed me that, from a larger cosmic perspective, my soul had selected these family members as teachers on its long multi-incarnation journey of growth. Despite all the drama I don't — I *can't* — regret anything. In this incarnation everything pulled me toward Buddhism, then plant shamanism, and eventually spiritual awakening.

How can I regret the events that led to my awakening, at last, inside this dream? A love now radiates through me, growing each day, like hot lava that conquers everything in its path.

* * *

Reflecting back, an incident stands out from my youth that I think about to this day, an early portent of what was to unfold much later.

I was 14 or 15 years old. One night it rained heavily, and I had a sleepless rest, interrupted by dreams. I rose in the morning, well before sunrise, dressed and crept quietly downstairs. I wrote an incantation of some sort on a piece of paper and left the house via the rear door. I folded the paper up and stuffed it in the stump of an old felled tree in our back yard, which was damp from nighttime rainfall.

I don't recall what I wrote — only that it felt important. What would possess me do such a thing?

I was on some kind of mission and felt compelled, summoned, to walk down the street and across a footbridge that connected our street to another neighborhood. With pinkish pre-dawn light illuminating the road, I made my way to the southeast corner of that area, where a single-story elementary school sprawled over a couple of acres. I walked over its mowed lawn and asphalt playgrounds to where the property terminated on a steep hillside high above the city's downtown core.

I sat down on a large damp rock, part of the ancient shoreline of what was once Lake Algonquin, carved by glaciers. I stared at the city below, whose residents were mostly still asleep. Then I watched the Sun rise, slowly, at first as a red crescent burning through the mist and eventually as a yellow-orange half-circle.

Then the most peculiar thing occurred: In a flash I saw the roundness of the Sun. It was not a flat disk but a fiery sphere. I comprehended its roundness and also experienced total awareness of its *true size*. At the same time I intuited its *actual distance* from the Earth! All in an instant, my consciousness grasped my position on this planet and the true size, scale and distance relationships between it and the rising Sun.

Then, most strangely, I became aware that the Sun is *conscious*. It's a conscious entity and in that moment it was as aware of me as I was aware of it.

This feeling dissipated as the Sun fully rose over the horizon and became too bright to look at directly. Things returned to normal, but something uncanny had happened. I'd received a transmission. Via some reality glitch the universe had let me know it is *sentient*, that everything is *alive*.

Satori! Oh!

CEREMONY 11

My eleventh and twelfth ayahuasca ceremonies occurred back-to-back over the Friday and Saturday nights of a single weekend in early April 2015. The location was a two-storey building in a snowy, forested area of rolling countryside in southern Ontario.

Providentially, the ceremonies were conducted under the auspices not only of a full moon, but also a lunar eclipse.

This weekend was special for a number of reasons, not the least being that my step-brother joined me — the first family member to try the ayahuasca medicine.

At the time Casey was a project management consultant, mostly working on contracts in the IT space. He typically managed institution-wide system launches for organizations like banks and stock brokerages. It was a demanding environment in which he coped well.

His coping was, and is, nuanced by the stress he retains from traumas he's carried into adult life from childhood. Our complex family constellation visited different gravitational pulls upon each of us — my step-brother, my sister and myself, sometimes pulling us so close to the Sun that it singed us, or flinging us out into the cold of interstellar space.

My stepbrother and I reconnected as adults, often during kayaking trips on the tiny islands of Georgian Bay that were medicine in themselves. We shared stories with one another of our various adventures into healing. We'd both tried many things over the years, including analysis, primal scream therapy, meditation, the Landmark Forum, and the escapist use of travel, sex, drugs and alcohol.

My guess is that between the two of us we'd pretty much done it all.

When I shared my initial stories about the "magic potion from the Amazon that solves all your problems," my stepbrother was intrigued, but showed no interest in trying it himself. When he was younger he'd experimented a few times with psychedelics like mushrooms and LSD. The results were generally less than constructive; like a child playing with a chemistry set, pouring liquids from one test tube into another had led to some explosions (figuratively speaking).

It sounded like the crucial "set and setting" had been poor. One time he walked around a busy area in an Asian city after drinking a too-large serving of mushroom tea, with strangers laughing at his white head that had just been shaved — a formula for a bad trip if there ever was one.

He became open to consuming an entheogenic plant in part because of the positive experience he and I shared in the summer of 2014 consuming mushrooms on our canoe trip in the Temagami wilderness. This went well because of the beautiful setting and also the respectful intention we brought.

And so, on this Friday in April, I left my dog with the dog-sitter and awaited my brother, who arrived by car at my condo mid-afternoon. Knowing we'd get little sleep that night, we went down for a short rest.

Early that evening — during the time we'd normally take dinner (which we skipped since we were fasting) — we set out as a two-car convoy and drove to the venue, which this time was in a woodsy area on the Niagara Escarpment.

On arrival, we unpacked our sleeping bags, pillows and overnight bags and lugged them to the large upstairs room that would become the ceremonial space. Most of the 20 or so pre-positioned floor mattresses were already occupied by an assortment of men and women who ranged widely in age and ethnicity. Most appeared to be in their twenties or thirties, with a few exuding that "I practice yoga" vibe.

My stepbrother took a spot near the top of the stairs. He used a sofa seat-cushion to create something comfortable to lean back on, as otherwise his backrest would have been the wooden uprights of the stair railing.

I chose the last remaining spot in the corner of the room, furthest away from the facilitators. This offered the advantage that no one would trip over me in the dark or accidentally kick my purge bucket.

We spent the next couple of hours socializing with the other guests in the ceremonial space and also in the small but adequately equipped downstairs kitchen. After stowing food I'd brought for the morning, I filled the electric kettle to make a cup of green tea that I sweetened with organic honey, then poured into a thermos for consumption near the end of the ceremony.

I changed into my white ceremonial clothing. I was going to pack my street clothes back in the car but decided instead to pre-position them on a hook in one of the washrooms downstairs, in case I wanted (or needed) something fresh to change into. *We were drinking ayahuasca, after all.*

By 9:00 p.m. we were all settled on our mattresses upstairs, most people lying back on pillows with blankets or with sleeping bags pulled over them. Recorded music played softly from an iPod stereo; it was the same song list I'd heard at a ceremony presided over by the same facilitators — Natasha and her friend — exactly a year prior (at a different location).

It gave me a warm feeling.

On my right side I positioned a folded-up yoga chair for later use, my purge bucket and other personal effects. To my left I placed a small brass statue of Ganesha that I'd purloined from my altar at home, and also a small orgone energy object (also from my altar). The orgone was a gift from Jun Jun, who was now living in Hawaii.

When I set the Ganesha statue on the floor, my neighbor — a young Russian woman — voiced her approval, apparently sharing my enthusiasm for the elephant-headed deity. Ganesha symbolizes clearing pathways for transformation (among other things), just like elephants remove trees in the forest for new growth.

Natasha and her friend were joined at the front of the room by an assistant facilitator — a young woman from Brazil who played the guitar and sang beautifully.

Earlier in the evening this woman had offered *rapé* to anyone who was interested. Rapé is a snuff made from tobacco and other ingredients that's sacred to the people of the Amazon. It's blown up the nose via a special V-shaped tube made from bone or other materials. Rapé is only mildly psychoactive and creates a light buzziness. I have come to appreciate it, but declined to consume it on this occasion, as I didn't want to potentiate the ayahuasca medicine in any way.

Natasha welcomed us all and, for the benefit of newcomers (some of whom had never drunk ayahuasca before), explained how the medicine is prepared and the rules for the evening.

For the newbies she added, *You should forget everything you've been told about ayahuasca, because your experience tonight will be unique to you.*

Sage advice.

She invited everyone to form a circle. We held hands and sang three long *Oms*. Then, from their mattresses, each person introduced themselves to the group and explained their intention for the night. With almost two-dozen people present, it took a long time to go around the room, especially because some people spoke at length.

I told the group my intention was to gain a deeper understanding of my path and how to more fully become the person Pachamama needs me to be.

I explained that I'd left my job at the end of the previous year. I mentioned that I was drawn to this particular ceremony in part to show support for Natasha, who I knew had endured a challenging year. And I commended my stepbrother for joining me in the ceremony. I told him there was nothing that his father (my stepdad) had faced on the battlefields of Korea or elsewhere that required more courage than what he was now undertaking.

The second facilitator smudged people one at a time with smoke from a small container of smoldering Palo Santo wood. Then each person took turns receiving their cup of ayahuasca.

I asked for, and received, a medium-size cup of the brown ayahuasca liquid, which I downed quickly to minimize exposure to its taste. Back on my mattress, I washed away the flavor with a very small amount of water from my canteen bottle.

After everyone drank, Natasha extinguished the candles and the room fell silent. We lay in the dark waiting for the medicine to come on.

Time passed slowly. I took advantage of my soon-to-end sober state to lie down fully and stretch out my back. I felt apprehensive about the hard work I knew awaited me. After what felt like about half an hour, one of the ayahuasceras started singing the first icaro of the night. Thus began one of my most memorable nights with the medicine.

Too much occurred in that one night to recount. At times it felt like I lived a month or even a lifetime in just a few hours. Time is far more elastic than people realize, and quantum physics suggests it may not exist at all. Instead, time may simply be an illusion conjured by consciousness to allow experience. One can enjoy, or be tormented in, stretches of time that vastly exceed the single night of a ceremony when journeying on ayahuasca medicine.

This was one of those nights when experiences felt like days or weeks or even months. Most of the experiences didn't survive as I re-crossed the event horizon of ordinary consciousness, but certain highlights stood out enough to make it into my field notes the next day.

One was the quality of the shamanic music and the women's voices. All three facilitators were very gifted at drumming and shaking the rattle, and each had an exquisite voice, as beautiful as that of any professional singer. Natasha and her friend possessed a good number of icaros. It was especially evident on this night that some songs were unique gifts from the plant kingdom. Others were traditional songs I'd heard sung by other facilitators.

At times songs were accompanied with a hand drum, and had a distinctly North American Indian inspiration. Some were sad laments sung in Portuguese or Spanish. Others — true *forest songs* — were enchanting, as though one were listening to a forlorn elvish queen calling through the mist.

It's impossible to convey to anyone who hasn't sat in ceremony the otherworldly quality of an authentic icaro heard under the influence of ayahuasca medicine.

I recognized one song in particular that I both enjoy and dread. I call it the "purge" song. Though it's not particularly unpleasant, something about it seems designed to make people vomit. It certainly has that affect on me, like a gravitational force exerted on my stomach. When I mentioned this to someone the following day, he knew exactly the song to which I was referring.

Of course, these songs stirred up the ayahuasca energy, but I found from the first cup I was not able to really break through. For the first hour I simply listened to the music in sober appreciation.

When the facilitators offered a second cup I was tempted to just lie there on my mattress and have a stress-free night.

Wasn't I there primarily to support my brother in his experience? I asked myself, trying to talk my way out of the situation. *God, but it would have been so great to just lie here*, I thought. *I can just pretend to be intoxicated and ride out the night with ease!*

But then I concluded, *Hell, I'm here anyway*, almost out loud.

Trepidatious of the hard work ahead, I walked to the altar and accepted a second cup. I noticed Natasha poured me only a tiny amount. Yet this was enough to push me over the edge. Soon after I returned to my mattress, a cascade of psychedelic visions overwhelmed me and I journeyed into the tryptamine space. (The next day Natasha mentioned she poured only a little the second time because she knew the action of simply walking across the room would be enough to activate the first cup. Such intuition!)

I spent the next three or four hours riding peaks and valleys of visionary and intuitive experience as the medicine came on or subsided in waves. The visions and insights more or less mapped the level of singing activity of the ayahuasceras.

Physically I felt slightly uncomfortable a lot of the time, though not unbearably so. I wasn't truly nauseous, but I kept adjusting into different positions to keep my stomach settled. At times I sat at the end of my mattress using my yoga chair for back support; other times I lay propped up on pillows or fully supine on my side.

I experienced my usual pattern of visual experience, starting with sacred geometry that appears first as a matrix of red and green lines against a black background, then vibrates and morphs into organic forms comprised of strobing lines in a rainbow of colors.

During this night the forms modulated almost ceaselessly between vegetative shapes (plant leaves, vines, tendrils) and animal forms (tentacles, reptilian or insect forms, legs, eyes, teeth, etc.). It's as though my consciousness was a tiny fish navigating the iridescent shoals of a phosphorous-lit coral reef at nighttime, with everything constantly evolving in new directions.

At times the vegetative forms — the tendrils or tentacles or coral tree branches — were lined with hundreds of tiny jewels or insect eyes.

I could influence the imagery, though I couldn't overpower it. At times it taunted me, or tried to terrify me or seduce me into dark places. I found I could play with it, dance with it, move it in different directions, and direct things upward into the light. Yes, I was dancing with the medicine now — with consciousness itself! — with me leading sometimes, and other times letting my partner lead. We improvised, broke into freestyle, came back together, danced formally, then free-styled again... always pushing, pushing, pushing, testing the limits...

Sometimes I'd deliberately ride the wave of a song down into dark inky fathoms where leviathan creatures lurk, then shoot upward, following rays of light toward something that felt like safety. I was a whale or dolphin swimming in a limitless ocean of consciousness.

Now I know why those mammals returned to the sea...

A constant theme was colored patterns with a distinctly Haida design. I don't know if the Haida Indians used entheogens, but I certainly felt I viewed *what they saw* when they were in some profound meditative state. I communed with the same source to which they found their way, somehow.

Though curanderos say these visual displays can become an empty "light show" if one forgets one's intention (rightly, I suppose), my experience was that these visions were the Divine showing herself to me in the most expansive way my limited human consciousness can comprehend — an extension of my own mind and a manifestation of God.

During the night the only exception to these beatific visions was one moment when the medicine perhaps sensed I was becoming over-confident, even cocky.

Do you want to feel what it's like to age? it railed at me in a terrifying voice. *Do you want to experience real death?*

It was aggressive and caused me to really pay attention.

No, I answered. I said this (in my mind) in a way that wasn't aggressive pushing back or simply dismissive. I simply chose that I didn't want to go down that path. This seemed to satisfy the medicine. I appeared to have passed some sort of test.

After a time, I don't know how long, I began to feel terribly ill. A seasick feeling ramped up quickly to the certain knowledge that something awful was brewing in my belly. I couldn't decide whether the storm was going to manifest as diarrhea or throwing up.

What would you like it to be? the plant voice asked.

I decided on vomiting. Within a few minutes I threw up violently into my purge bucket, making loud retching and gasping sounds that I knew people would hear all across the room.

It was cosmic!

It only lasted a few minutes and then I was done. From that moment on I felt absolutely amazing, for the rest of the night and for the rest of the weekend.

On this occasion I felt that at least some of what I threw up were my brother's issues, though I was (and remain) unsure. Perhaps I "took one for the team" much as I had in the previous ceremony where dark eyes had welled up in my purge bucket.

Eventually the facilitators sang the popular hymn *Om Namah Shivaya* accompanied by an Indian drone harmonium. In the same way as happened when they had sung it the previous year, I went straight to heaven, surrounded by pink glowing light, in a state of ecstasy, with tears welling up in the face of sacred beauty.

I asked that it never stop!

Soon after, at the latter stage of the ceremony, I received a major teaching that presented itself in an uncanny way.

All the psychedelic stuff faded and in a large square area in the center of my visual plane I saw a vignette that looked like a shaky old Super 8 home movie.

It was my mother, Yvonne, playing golf. She was wearing a golf visor and her eyes beamed. She was clearly enjoying herself, and I was able to look closely at her eyes. They were directing love and attention toward some person "off camera."

It was startlingly realistic.

Sometimes it's difficult to conjure up a detailed recollection of a person's face. We think we can do it, but if you stop and try, randomly, it's actually difficult to reconstruct a person's features in great detail, even of close relatives. (Sometimes people get upset after a loved one dies, castigating themselves that they can't remember what they looked like.) But in this instance I saw my mother as if she were right in front of me. It was a sunny day and she was happy.

After this vision disappeared I lay back and contemplated what it meant.

It was very strange. To start with, my mother doesn't play golf. In the vision she appeared younger than her age at the time of the vision — perhaps in her late forties, I'd guess.

Then I figured it out, and the realization hit me hard.

The universal consciousness was showing me my mother enjoying another life — a different life than the one she chose.

In this other life, she'd married someone other than my father. I was seeing her enjoying herself with other people in a world into which I'd never been born, a world in which she was not my mother.

There are few things more painful than seeing your own mother enjoying a life in which she never became your mom.

All at once I felt the poignancy of our bond as it (thankfully) exists, and the "near miss" of my never having been born.

Why I was being shown this was self-evident: It was all about appreciation, and I felt gratitude. Immense gratitude.

We focus so much on the various ways our parents fail or disappoint us, without appreciating enough our good fortune in ever having landed a place in the realm of the embodied in the first place.

I was then taken on a whirlwind tour of her marriages to her first and second husbands. I got to see how the universe conspired to create me. Even the toughest experiences I endured growing up — the emotional abandonment or abuse I felt at times — was all part of a program to prepare me for my destiny.

It's impossible to fully convey the nuance of this lesson. In the end, the lesson was for me, and for me only. It wasn't some kind of intellectualization either, but more of a felt experience. I found myself longing... longing for *what actually happened*...

I ended the night feeling a softening in my heart and thankfulness to the universe for my simply *being*. There'd been so much preparation I'd never understood before. It was strange, seeing the mysterious plan Pachamama had for me.

In time the formal part of the ceremony concluded with the facilitators coming round to each of us, leaning in to blow mapacho tobacco smoke on the crown of our heads, between our folded hands, and on our chests and backs.

I opened my thermos and sipped the tea I'd prepared the evening before. The ceremony had been long and the tea had cooled. After a few sips I wandered downstairs to the kitchen and made myself a fresh batch, feeling steady on my feet but still lightly in the thrall of the medicine.

Tea in hand, I put on my coat, shoes and cap, and walked out into the cold night air, onto the veranda from which I stared at the brilliant silver disk of the moon as it emerged from the clouds. The moon showered her pale white light through the upraised branches of the leafless trees and illuminated the snow-covered fields of a nearby copse.

The silence staggered me, as did the trees that stood like sentinels.

I soon felt chilled and went back upstairs to the warm ceremonial room and lay down on my mattress. Everyone retired for the night on their mats; eventually the room was illuminated only slightly by the blue light of the iPod stereo from which soft Indian music emanated. I drifted off to sleep with faint shimmering red and green geometric lines dancing behind my eyelids.

* * *

In the morning I awoke before most of the others and joined a few early risers in the kitchen, where they were busy making tea and coffee.

I poured myself some hot water and made instant coffee from a package of individual pouches I'd brought. I then used the washroom. Everything was normal with my digestive system.

Thank heaven for small mercies, I thought.

By the time I returned upstairs, coffee in hand, the group was ready to start sharing, and again we went around the room slowly as each person described their nights — some difficult, some gentle, a few something in-between. I gave the best account I could of my experiences and enjoyed the others' sharing.

My stepbrother told his story, first focusing on form, then content. His stomach had troubled him throughout the night but I was pleased to learn he'd received a fairly significant teaching. It related to how he holds on to damaging experiences from the past and needs to let them go. This presented itself as a fascinating visual experience in which his memories of past traumas were stored in boxes that he lugged with him everywhere, each one containing a kind of demented clown, like a scary Jack-in-the-box.

After the sharing we all descended downstairs for a communal meal. I thought it was sad that we don't build apartment complexes to allow this sort of thing on a regular basis.

Later that morning my brother conveyed to me that, worthwhile as everything had been, he'd decided to not stay for the second night. He was okay with losing his deposit for the second ceremony.

I was disappointed but told him I understood. I was thankful he had come at all, and I was aware that two ceremonies held back-to-back can be daunting for people the first time they drink. I was just happy he was initiated into the realm of the plant teachers.

I managed to sleep for a few hours that afternoon. When Saturday evening came around I again made a cup of tea and walked upstairs to my mattress. I noticed I wasn't as trepidatious as usual. I had an intuition that this night would be a gentle one, or at least that's what I hoped.

14

The concern of the Primary Imagination, its only concern, is with sacred beings and events... A sacred being cannot be anticipated; it must be encountered... All imaginations do not recognize the same sacred beings or events, but every imagination responds to those it recognizes in the same way... The response of the imagination... is a passion of awe.

— W.H. Auden

As evening fell I lay on my mat, thinking about the previous night's ceremony, and the one that was about to start.

It wasn't lost on me that this would be my twelfth ceremony, and I thought about its significance. The number 12 is sacred, appearing in ancient myths and religion. One example is Christ and his 12 apostles.

All of that goes back to ancient astronomy. Twelve is a factor of 72 — the number of years it takes for the Sun and stars in certain Zodiac constellations to move one degree as they cross the horizon during the equinoxes and solstices.

As Giorgio de Santillana and Hertha von Dechend demonstrate in *Hamlet's Mill* — their book on archaeoastronomy — ancient people faithfully observed the precession of the equinoxes — the 26,000-year cycle that's sometimes called the Great Year. If we divide 26,000 years by the 360 degrees in a circle, we get the number 72.

Thus we are entering the Age of Aquarius as that constellation gradually displaces Pisces at the equinox sunrise.

Although I wouldn't finalize the decision until later, my mind held glimmerings that my twelfth ayahuasca ceremony would be an appropriate one to end on, at least for this cycle of working with the plant medicine.

I'd already received messages during the most recent ceremonies that it was perhaps time for me to take a break. I had much integration work to do.

What? Not you again! the medicine seemed to exclaim at times. *Haven't I given you enough work to do?*

And so it was with a sense of finality that I prepared myself mentally for that evening's events. The facilitators entered the ceremonial space and the event got under way.

CEREMONY 12

The second evening's ceremony began exactly as the night before, with instructions from Natasha, our singing three Oms as a group, and the offering of protection with the Palo Santo smudge.

Many of the guests from the first night remained, but there were some new faces and introductions to be made. I felt vaguely sad that my brother wasn't there, more from a sense of what he might be missing than any difference it might make to my experience.

In the sharing circle I said I wanted a *night of integration* and to go deeper into *learning my path*.

Although I didn't say it at the time, I was also interested in asking the universal consciousness to show me what elephants experience in the wild, from *their* perspective. In other ceremonies I'd experienced reality from the perspective of other creatures such as insects and amphibians.

It had been very warm in the ceremony room the night before and I'd sweated in my white ceremonial clothing. I didn't want to wear anything unclean, so for this evening I changed into a pair of orange cotton pants I'd bought in Peru that bore a black serpent Shipibo design, and a blue cotton shirt with a print illustration of Ganesha on the front. In addition to being very comfortable, this supported my interest in elephants that night.

I replaced the black dragon bracelet I normally wore on my left wrist (a favorite piece a girlfriend bought for me in Mexico) with a sparkling gold serpent bracelet my mother had brought home for me from a trip to India.

On my right wrist I replaced the spiral bracelet I'd worn the night before (featuring small Mexican Day of the Dead skulls) with a silver bracelet with a green glass sphere in the center. I wore brass rings with Sanskrit prayers embossed on them, and a snake ring on my right pinkie finger that had an actual piece of ayahuasca embedded in it.

These talismans were to comfort me during my night's journey, or so I hoped.

When it was my turn to attend the altar I assumed I'd receive a similar portion of the same medicine as the night before, because I'd discussed this with Natasha.

How about we try this instead? she said, as she produced a different bottle (white in color) and proceeded to pour a serving that filled about three quarters of the small cup.

That's fine, I said. *I trust you.*

It tasted similar to the other ayahuasca but, if pressed, I'd say it tasted like it had been filtered more; it seemed to have less sediment. I imagined I'd been served some kind of extra special medicine, and the visions that followed seemed to confirm that guess.

It's difficult to describe the night that followed because it was quite long and had a lot going on. I'd summarize it as simply being *in the presence of the Divine,* much as happened in my eighth ayahuasca ceremony.

The visual experience was similar to the previous night with the difference being, perhaps, the level of clarity and also the amount of light. Yes, it was very light-filled, and in fact I spent a long time following a brilliant light as white and as intense as the Sun (except that I could look directly at it). This may have been the same essence of consciousness that inspired the iconoclastic Pharaoh Akhenaten to re-imagine Egyptian religion as a monotheism based on worshipping the Sun, or *Aten*. His ideas were so radical that after his death the city he built was abandoned, his monuments were demolished, and subsequent rulers did everything they could to erase his name and ideas from history.

The strange white light moved up and up into gossamer realms and I moved toward it inexorably, much as a fish might follow the sun from below the surface of rippling water.

Was this some kind of kundalini energy? I wondered.

Again I saw hundreds of visions made up of strobing light and rainbow color. This night everything was sped up a bit, too. Things changed faster and faster and sometimes I thought to open my eyes and just "turn it all off" (which was something I'd practiced doing the night before).

But a voice seemed to say, *Just lie back and relax.*

You worked hard last night and purged. You're purified now. Just watch and learn, and try to remember what you see.

So that's what I did for most of the next couple of hours. I felt the medicine more than ever as a true ally.

As the night wore on I pressed the teacher plant to answer my questions about elephants. She seemed to tell me I could investigate that for myself, but after I persisted she told me about their world. I was disappointed that I wasn't shown what the world looks like *through their eyes*. Instead, the medicine told me (rather than showed me) that they have an unusual hybrid way of both looking ahead (like predators) and to both sides (like prey animals).

I was told about their social organization, which is a kind of monarchy with kings and queens, and handmaidens or ladies in waiting. I was shown the role of the male elders and the importance of their rank and social position, and the way the matriarchs rule the families and raise the young. Very much as we've been told, they have an ancient culture and remember their dead and mourn them. They live in kingdoms and their social position is important to them.

I asked Pachamama if she could share any insights into why they're being killed and got a pretty matter of fact answer, along the lines of *do the math.*

I lay on my mat contemplating this challenge.

It costs money to protect elephants; people make money killing them (for their ivory). In a human world in which everything is valued in strict consumerist terms, elephants are more valuable dead than alive.

This lesson morphed into an overview of how human beings and their extractive industries are in conflict with nature, which ought to be valued just for itself. Instead of taking the very least possible, capitalism rewards companies for taking the very most. Our inability to appreciate the wild and simply leave it alone is drawing down whole ecosystems.

You can worry about the elephants if you like, but it's you humans who are going extinct, and you don't see it, ayahuasca said.

This caught me off guard and was followed by a stern comment.

The time of humans is ending.

There was a fierceness in this message, which was spat out with snake energy. It appeared Gaia has pretty much had enough of us and what we're doing to every other creature on the planet.

I asked something like, *But aren't we special to you? We are unique.*

To which the answer was (words to the effect) that, yes, we are unusual, but we're no more special to her than other creatures. She's the awareness in every being. She gets immense pleasure from being slithering snakes, and scorpions, and spiders, and even those cockroaches we're so fond of saying will rule the Earth after we've destroyed everything.

I am both the lion and the gazelle, she said, reminding me of earlier ceremonies in which I was allowed insights into her being both the lion's pleasure in pulling down its prey as well as the prey's terror in being caught. The yin-yang of all things.

I will live on through the tiniest insect or the most obscure creatures on the bottom of the ocean, she said telepathically. I intuited that other life will evolve on this planet in new forms, just as it has over and over again after previous extinction events. Gaia told me she's busy on other planets, too. Some of my visions that night were of strange jellyfish life forms in other parts of the universe that float in the sky.

I felt quite desperate from the lesson about *the time of humans ending*, but things became ambiguous, as happens often in shamanic experience.

At the very same time one part of my brain was processing the foreboding message, I was listening to the icaros and, at just the right moment, alternative signals were conveyed about hope. The songs were an invitation to trust in nature, to listen to the heartbeat of the planet. The lyrics contained crucial information about healing Earth and how to get out of this mess. I became painfully aware of how few people are available to make the difference and shift the balance.

Mother Nature needs every last one! There are many of *them*, I intuited — meaning the unconscious destroyers — and very few of *us*.

I flirted with sleep in the latter part of the night, never quite passing out.

As the ceremony wound down and we received our tobacco blessings, I thought about all the work I have to do sharing information to bring about change. It was all quite overwhelming and I didn't know what to do next. I knew only that important work awaited.

This is what I shared with the group the following morning in our circle, after we slept until about 9:00 a.m. Then we convened casually downstairs again for breakfast.

I had an interesting conversation with the co-facilitator from Quebec. She told me stories of spirit quests she's undertaken in the wilderness under the supervision of First Nations elders in which, she said, other people ate and drank on her behalf.

You can go for days without being hungry, she said, *if others eat and drink for you.*

She told me that animals come forward and you can communicate with them telepathically, like deer and even wolves. One time a skunk sat beside her and was no threat, because of the connected state she was in.

She told me a fascinating story of people she'd met in Mexico who live without eating food. I asked her how they survive and she answered,

By staring at the Sun at sunrise, when it's okay to look without your eyes burning.

This was the first time I heard of breatharians. This also reminded me of that episode when I was a teenager, watching the sun rise and feeling it was in communication with me.

She said one woman carried two pregnancies to full term without food, not having eaten in 15 years, and the babies were born healthy. She said the claims have been independently verified, after I asked if she didn't think these people snuck out sometimes and grabbed a bite to eat somewhere.

Needing to liberate my dog from the sitter I eventually packed my things, hauled them out to the car, and departed.

I felt an immediate nostalgia driving away. I'm always a bit sad after such gatherings, Ah! To have become so close to so many people, to have shared such mysteries, and then to just drive away, possibly never to see one another again...

My ayahuasca ceremonies caused me to long for real community. Modern urban life is indeed harsh and dehumanizing, even when our homes and apartments are comfortable.

Yet as I drove away I also felt immense gratitude for having dwelled in the presence of the Divine (for so many hours!) and for being shown the path forward, even if I couldn't see past all the curves ahead.

Blood is effectively a magnetohydrodynamic plasma for light. Hemoglobin's peak absorptions telegraph this... and the fact that aromatic amino acids are the favorite amino acids in construction of the blood should be a tell too.

— Dr. Jack Kruse

Much happened soon after that twelfth ayahuasca ceremony.

Many were processes understandable via the intellectual framework of Freudian or Jungian psychology.

Through the clinical lens, ayahuasca had revisited me to childhood's and other traumas, for renegotiation from an adult perspective of the emotional impact of disturbing events in earlier times. New neural pathways were laid down, allowing the emotional component of my psychology and even my sympathetic nervous system to access different strategies to not only survive but *thrive*.

Certain addictive tendencies such as an over-fondness for alcohol vanished, or were at least greatly reduced. Patterns that might have re-emerged as multi-month or year-long cycles of alcohol overindulgence or depression now exhausted themselves in a few days. Or even hours.

From a spiritual perspective, Amazonian plant medicine had the net effect of being an accelerant. In time I came to appreciate that the visions in themselves had less lasting effect than having encountered over and over again my deepest Self, and this went far further than a psychiatric version of such notions: I had encountered the Brahma or Atman consciousness, unmitigated.

As I returned to ordinary conscious states, an evermore calm and Zen-like detachment pervaded my being. I came to appreciate the integration work that people always talk about in ayahuasca circles. For me, this required that I revisit and cultivate Buddhist insights, and not fall back into the old ways. I felt vaccinated against the drama that arises when passing thoughts and emotions are confused with one's true identity.

I worked at remembering and implementing the lessons, as I called them, but not fetishizing the visions. When I attended social gatherings of people interested in ayahuasca, I noticed a certain evangelical spirit among some participants. Fresh off the plane from Peru, they extolled the healing power of the plants and told wild-eyed stories of their visions. I was something of an evangelist myself, when still in what a friend of mine calls the *honeymoon phase* of the ayahuasca relationship. In time I settled down, returning fully to the yoga of ordinary life, finding magic in the mundane world, which is not mundane at all.

I gained clarity about my life's purpose, which (ironically) is a renewed *purposelessness*. But, like many purposeless-yet-awakened people, I wanted to be of service. There wasn't really *anything else to do*.

Things had come full circle and I was back, in some ways, to where I started. I felt an inevitable *drop*, as people often do when they return home from invigorating retreats. I wondered sometimes what the crazy Year of Drinking Magic had accomplished.

Yet, as Terry Pratchett writes, returning isn't the same as never having gone away.

My heart was opened, and remains open.

And I knew the mind to be a trickster. I still had to live with my mind, of course, but now we were roommates and not a couple trapped in an unwanted sadomasochistic relationship. Instead of tying one another up and tormenting each other, we met each morning for tea on the patio, enjoying the early sun.

Things might have remained just like that, and to some extent they have, but inevitably I was haunted by further questions.

I'd already concluded that I both agreed and disagreed with Buddhism writer Brad Warner about psychedelics. My experience of them had been (unlike Warner's) immensely positive. I felt that if I could be a good non-attached Buddhist in ordinary reality, I could be a good non-attached Buddhist in altered states as well. Yet I agreed with what I assume Warner would forewarn, about making too much of the experiences, clinging to the visions themselves, and seeking for ways to hang out in that other dimension too often.

Had I experienced true enlightenment? Or only a false one?

I recognized the risk in thinking enlightenment was always just *one ceremony away*, or that being with God required being in a state curated by plant intermediaries.

Another way I began to think of it was, *Is it possible to experience ordinary reality as psychedelic? All the time?*

Not from being *high* — at least not from a drug or plant — but from feeling the high of Oneness with God (or the universe), always?

I knew this was something Ram Dass had thought upon deeply when he went to and returned from India. Dass had said being fully present was key, along with an attitude of compassion. And I knew from Alan Watts' lectures it would include a quality of ever-present playfulness, an in-the-moment flowing like water. This was easy for me to grasp, now, as it became my state of being. I put concepts into dynamic action that used to be mere intellectualizations.

Speaking of "intellectualizations," I encountered a phenomenon that took some getting used to, and that is *intellectual naysayers*. I hadn't anticipated (but should have been prepared for) the battery of people who attempted to gaslight my experiences with plant shamanism. This was not restricted only to people unfamiliar with ayahuasca or other teacher plants, whose ignorance was understandable. Their concerns were easy to brush off and were actually quaint. The more problematic naysayers were the people experienced with psychedelics, be they mushrooms or other plants, or drugs like LSD. Some of these folks were educated and very intelligent. Their admonitions stung — that I was just fooling myself about spiritual encounters with the numinous. They were all "in my head," they'd say, and commonplace to anyone consuming psychotropic substances.

In time I came to understand that people who say these things are themselves "stuck in their head" and have not experienced a true heart opening. Authentic spiritual experience is not just cerebral, but visceral and of the heart-mind. Their need to discredit the spiritual experience of others reflects where they've stopped on their own path. But when I first encountered this attitude, I wasn't strong in my "knowing," which condensed more fully later.

Knowing I had more work to do, my thoughts turned to investigating which ongoing relationships with shamanic visionary plants — and shamanism itself (with or without plants) — would support my shiny new awakened life?

I wasn't asking these questions in a vacuum. Shamanism had fished me into her boat and I hadn't been released back into the water!

Powerful dreams intruded upon my sleep, and I often woke up at 4:00 in the morning to visions of sacred geometry dancing behind my eyelids. Auroras of white light appeared, and short remote-viewing incidents of landscapes in other times or places.

For strangeness, nothing beat the ongoing visits from my spirit animal. The white snake continued to show up at different times of the day or night, forcing me to stop what I was doing as it grew in size from a tiny point of light until it filled my field of vision and entered my head.

Eventually I realized I was viewing it from the very center of my consciousness; it was not external and wasn't coming from somewhere outside.

I am the animal, and it is me, I realized. And I was certainly viewing it with my awakened Third Eye.

As the depth of my knowing crystallized, I sought out the Canadian tribal tattoo artist Damien Rowanchilde to inscribe the magical serpent on my left arm, in celebration of my beautiful and life-affirming relationship with this emissary of The Mysterium.

My inner and outer worlds increasingly became the same, everything quantumly entangled.

My experience of the 11:11 phenomenon continued, and other odd synchronicities that felt like hints from the universe, guiding me back to my path.

The 11:11 phenomenon was something I'd never heard about until it started happening to me, which added to its mystery and power. It wasn't as if I'd seen it on TV and then went looking for it! Those numbers started showing up all the time in striking ways. The important thing about the phenomenon, I learned, is not just noticing the numbers, but what you're *thinking about* when they show up.

For example, one day when I was apartment-sitting my stepbrother's condominium in downtown Toronto, I walked from his place to Yonge Street, thinking about how it had been a while since I'd done anything identifiably spiritual. As I turned the corner onto Yonge Street I noticed a large sign in a shop window beside me of a man holding the numbers 11:11. It was a Pizza Pizza store, and the numbers were part of the chain's famous advertising jingle that repeats the phone number 967-11-11.

More strikingly, I checked the time on my phone. It was 11:11 a.m.

That evening I decided to walk to a local pub. As I made my way down my brother's street my thoughts turned to the mysterious ways in which the universe communicates, and whether or not I was just kidding myself, as a hardcore materialist naysayer would no doubt say. Just then I looked up and saw a full moon beaming down on me. Then looking up and to my left, I noticed a single window lit up from inside the otherwise dark apartment block beside me, in which stood a statue of Buddha, looking up smiling with his arms up-stretched toward the moon.

Strange! I thought. But things got stranger still.

I turned the corner and continued along the next street. A few minutes later I was thinking about the incident with the Pizza Pizza sign from earlier that day, asking myself almost out loud, *I wonder how many different ways the 11:11 phenomenon can manifest itself?* At precisely that moment a man leaned out toward me from beneath a restaurant awning and said, *One, One, One, One* before leaning back into the shadows.

Such synchronicities have continued in my life, and seem to multiply during the times when I make good decisions around evolving my consciousness toward love and understanding.

* * *

After my twelfth ceremony my ayahuasca work slowed down.

I attended one ceremony offered by Bolormaa and Tiger at a mutual friend's house, which recapitulated all the themes of my first dozen ceremonies. The lessons repeated themselves and the plant spirit itself seemed to be saying, *I have no more lessons for you until you've done more work in ordinary reality.*

My friend Bobbi invited me to attend a couple of Santo Daime ceremonies, which use a variation of ayahuasca (the daime) similar to the one with which I was familiar, though it was thinner and its effects wore off more quickly.

The first of my experiences with this Brazilian syncretic church took place in a municipal facility in Toronto that the city rents out for various kinds of events. The *work* (as such ceremonies are called) was held during the day on an important calendar date near Easter. I joined the men lined up on one side of an informal altar facing the women on the other side, and we sang Christian songs in Portuguese from little hymnbooks for about seven hours. We stood almost the whole time, dancing in patterned steps.

This would have been demanding and exhausting in itself, but when the medicine hit, it was mind-bendingly challenging (which is the point). Imagine line dancing on LSD for seven hours and you get the idea.

At one point I became very fed up with the whole thing and excused myself to the bathroom, where I sat on the toilet plotting my escape.

What a stupid mistake this was! I thought. *I can't stand another minute of this!*

I started planning to sneak out the side door and drive away, but then remembered I was high on the medicine and in no condition to drive.

As I sat there seething, the singing filtered up the stairs and down the hall to where I was, and gradually a feeling came over me that I should go back down and at least fulfill my obligation to complete this day's work.

I actually imagined myself as the Grinch Who Stole Christmas up in his mountain lair, scowling down at the Whos in Whoville, holding hands and singing in a circle. I instantly received a lesson: I'd just caught a powerful glimpse of my own ego mind. That little tin-pot dictator Grinch was used to getting his way, drawing me away from community, collective effort and joy.

I returned downstairs and finished the long afternoon *work*, standing the whole time, dancing and singing with gusto. When the daime waned I drank another cup and felt supported by a wondrous field of energy generated by the group; I appreciated the shaman-less alternate tradition very much, though in the end it didn't feel right for me (for the long term).

I attended one more time, in that instance a *concentração* (meditation-style) work that took place in the late afternoon at another facility. This event was similar to the other one, but shorter, and it differed in that it included several long periods in which we sat in silence, meditating while in the thrall of the daime.

The metal chairs weren't terribly comfortable but, as I'd been advised, I wedged a thin cushion behind my back and another on my seat to make things tolerable. In truth, I was happy to be seated at all, after the other standing ceremony.

I sat in the subdued lighting and noticed quantum-level patterns on the white shirt sleeves and black vests of the men seated in front of me.

The DMT in the daime is certainly at work, I thought to myself.

We sat twice during the overall ceremony. The first time I reviewed the profound insights I'd had during my various ayahuasca ceremonies. Thinking of the naysayers and their admonitions, I told the daime medicine that these felt like enlightenment experiences, but that I wondered if it might not be some kind of mental game. I was confused about what was real, and feared the dreaded *false enlightenment,* via which the ego mind tricks a person into thinking he or she has attained liberation, only as a ploy to maintain the ego's ongoing supremacy.

How do I know that the visions and insights you're showing me now, I asked the daime, *aren't some kind of trick also? How can I discern the real thing?*

I feared this was a bit brash on my part and braced myself for a stern ayahuasca-style lesson, but then the medicine began to wear off quickly.

Oh no! I said, in my mind. *You haven't answered me yet!*

Don't worry! the daime answered. *The night is still young.*

And that was true: several more hours of ceremony remained. After more dancing we were invited up for a second cup and soon after we sat down in our chairs for another *concentração.*

Okay, I thought. *Now we can get back to my question about real versus false enlightenment.*

No sooner had I completed that thought, than the daime gave me my answer, in the most enthralling way.

A surge of energy flowed through my body all of a sudden, like I'd stepped on the third rail of an underground subway train. Except the energy didn't flow through my *foot.* Instead, it flowed through my *heart.*

I teared up and struggled to not fall off my chair as a reverie came over me — an ecstasy and joy that defies description.

The daime didn't need to say anything telepathically. I got the lesson immediately: Real awakening is a matter of the heart and not the brain. This Divine love that poured through me like a tsunami was the talisman of authentic Self-realization. We are, when all is said and done, pure love, and nothing else.

As I lay in bed that night, still brimming with this sense of cosmic unity, I realized I'd spent years seeking enlightenment with my mind, trapped in the ego's house of mirrors where I'd wondered if each reflection was the real me.

Lead with the heart, I realized, *and I will never be deceived.*

* * *

After the daime works I stepped away from all shamanic plants for a while, but eventually felt drawn to try some other plants. I was motivated by curiosity and also because I wondered if there was a way to connect to the Divine through plant intermediaries without it being as harrowing as the vine of souls or as demanding as the dancing and Portuguese hymns of the daime.

My experiments with mushrooms had been promising in that regard.

My last ayahuasca ceremonies had included a shamanic death element, in which I felt increasingly that I was in the place of pure consciousness from which we emerge at birth and to which we return when we die.

Was it possible, I wondered, to enter a state of Oneness without going to that intimidating place?

Things were not as cut and dried schedule-wise as I've suggested.

In the summer of 2014 — and again in the autumn of 2015 — I had the opportunity to work with *huachuma* — the sacred visionary plant of the Inca — whose use had survived in the high Andes. Sadly, the traditions and beliefs surrounding the use of this plant are almost completely lost, as the priests who facilitated the traditions, and any written materials about it, were destroyed centuries ago by the Spanish.

Huachuma is also known as San Pedro cactus — St. Peter being, appropriately, the guardian of the gates to heaven. The plant is similar in its properties to the better-known peyote cactus, with mescaline being the main psychedelic component.

My first experience with huachuma took place with a small group of people at a location outside Ottawa, Ontario in a forest setting on the Canadian Shield. The area — Carp — is famously the home of an underground bunker complex built during the height of the Cold War, known as the Emergency Government Headquarters museum or the "Diefenbunker."

In an extremely ironic contrast, the area is also considered a place of almost dangerous levels of magical power by its original First Nations inhabitants, who tend to steer clear of it.

Sitting on blankets and pillows in a clearing, a bit trepidatious about distant rainclouds, we spent a glorious day in the forest, bathed in sweet music from the musicians in attendance. These included a Quebecois man who was an excellent improvisational guitar player, and a woman (also from Quebec) who was a consummate violinist. Their collaboration throughout the day on a variety of spontaneous melodies greatly enhanced what became a glorious and ineffable encounter with the Divine in nature.

It's difficult to convey the effects of huachuma. A clue is its being called the *ayahuasca of the day*, or the *medicine of light*. I was reminded of the scenes in James Cameron's film *Avatar* when the main protagonist sees the spirits in plants, vines and the great tree that the foreign mining company eventually pulls down.

In addition to a warm glow, I could see a flickering light inside each plant and tree of the surrounding forest.

At one point, lying back, the medicine voice said, *Why don't you try taking off your glasses?*

When I did, the forest canopy above me immediately became a network of snakes — green where the tree leaves filled my visual space, and blue where there were patches of sky.

I naturally recoiled, remembering the intensity of snakes during ayahuasca ceremonies. But the snakes immediately — and comically — set my mind at ease by exclaiming, *Don't worry! We're nice snakes! We're going to have lots of fun today!*

And this turned out to be the case.

Huachuma is also called the Grandfather medicine, and the second time I drank it — this time in a forest north of Toronto — the plant spirit appeared to me as masculine and elderly. It was like a grandfather who tugs your ear and teases you not to take things so seriously, especially yourself.

I received a lesson in seeing, related to losing (then finding) my glasses among the leaves, and experienced a great heart opening in which compassion flooded into me and through me for the men who've most impacted my life, especially my late father and stepfather. It was like the lessons about the Mother with ayahuasca, but this time the teachings concerned the Father.

* * *

On a Saturday in July, 2016 I attended a party on the Toronto waterfront aboard a cruise boat named the River Gambler hosted by Lovelution — a conscious dance party organization co-founded by my friend

Michael Sanders — author of the book *Ayahuasca: An Executive's Enlightenment* that I helped edit. I'd been to several of the land-based Lovelution parties and enjoyed their combination of New Age rave and post-apocalyptic *Mad Max* vibe. Unsurprisingly, Sanders and his partners in Lovelution are veteran Burning Man attendees.

The boat cruise version, which took place from around noon until 5:00 pm, was about the same, but with water and changing scenery. A preternaturally good-looking and fit crowd of young men and women dominated the scene.

I arrived with a friend who's a model, hula-hoop dancer, vegan chef and a bunch of things that qualified her as a good candidate for the dance-your-face-off scene. Shortly before we arrived I changed into some dance clothing and a meter-wide leather sombrero my older son had given me as a birthday present. He likely thought I'd never wear it, but I was dancing life now like never before.

We were searched and patted down by security as we boarded the ship, but my contraband (psilocybin mushrooms in capsule form) escaped detection. I envisioned myself dancing the afternoon away on the upper deck, with perhaps some colors, lights and geometric patterns seeping into my visual perception.

I ate two capsules, which I considered a mild dose. But when the medicine came on, it sent me into a full-on ayahuasca-type journey. Within a few minutes it was obvious I needed to lie down.

I made my way to the back of the ship and down the metal staircase to the deck below, the interior of which was set up artfully with different areas for massage tables, fortune readings and other activities. One area was covered in mats and rugs, on which people lounged or sat talking in small groups.

I found a black beanbag chair in the corner and sprawled across it.

At this point the ordinary 3D world of my visual field was switched out for another one made up of a diamond-cut semi-translucent landscape of moving and changing forms with strobing colors and jewel-like Faberge egg decoration, exactly as I'd seen on ayahuasca. This experience lasted for approximately the next three or four hours, peaking at about the 90-minute mark after onset, but maintaining a high level of intensity until about 30 minutes before the boat returned to port.

In addition to the visual experience, I received many teachings from the plant, including a reminder that there is no such thing, for me, as a "small dose" of psychedelic plants. I can never use these plants recreationally.

The telepathic plant voice was both stern and somewhat amused about how it had ensnared me. I felt deliberately tricked.

Wave after wave of visions washed over me, with the whole room disappearing at times, I sometimes felt a fly bite me and realized we were somewhere in the channels of the Toronto Islands. I was saddened that I was missing the party, but this was trivial in comparison with the experience that overwhelmed me.

I endured a series of rapid-fire shamanic deaths in which I died, came back again, died, and came back again, over and over. This went on for a very long time. When I couldn't stand it any more and began to worry about possibly not coming back at all, I forced myself to sit up.

I sat in a daze, contemplating the fact that, forevermore, psilocybin mushrooms would foment an ayahuasca-like journey. This was daunting but valuable, as it meant I could *go to that place* without having to find and consume the Amazonian plant.

I processed also that these plants are, for me, a new category that I began to call *necroptics* — a term I adapted from biologist Rupert Sheldrake. They transport me to the realm of the departed, not only engendering visions of that place but also simulating near death experiences (NDEs), the effects of which include extremely shallow breathing and a slowed pulse. The medicines appear to bring me as close as possible to actually dying, pushing me literally over that brink until I lose consciousness and stop breathing. After some time — which I can't measure because I'm out cold — my body lurches with a pre-programmed survival response and I wake up with a great gasping for air, and then the process continues.

Needless to say, when people invite me to come over and *share some 'shrooms* recreationally, I decline. They don't realize they may as well be saying, *Hey Guy! Would you like to come over and experience exhausting simulated death for a few hours?*

On the boat I eventually I found myself talking with a young man and woman. Our conversation was mostly me channeling what the plant medicine wanted to convey. The experience became oracular. I viewed both the man and woman in their human 3D incarnation and also as their divine selves. It was the oddest thing seeing the woman's face toggling back and forth between that of an ordinary attractive twenty-something and an eternal goddess with features like the Madonna in Michelangelo's *First Pieta*.

I recall sharing with them that the universe is like a giant Etch-A-Sketch that God shakes, eliminating the design in each go-round. The Etch-A-Sketch has been shaken thousands of times before. Through me the plant spoke about a range of matters concerning death and illusion; I was as much part of the audience as the people beside me.

When it felt right to end the discussion I thanked the couple for their indulgence and they thanked me and went on their way. Self-conscious that maybe I'd made an ass of myself, I contacted them a few days later by phone and they reassured me it was all just as profound as I'd imagined.

On the last leg of the drive home, after I dropped off my friend, a large bird of prey — a hawk — flew across my car windshield at a distance of only a few feet. This felt portentous.

Another synchronicity, I thought to myself as I finished the drive home. I had never seen a hawk in the city before.

* * *

I was pleased to know a neural pathway connected me to the realm of souls, for which the gateway was now easily obtained psilocybin mushrooms, and that the huachuma medicine offered a daytime version of ayahuasca that was light-filled and (for me) completely non-harrowing.

I became interested in experiencing something I'd first learned about from Rick Strassman's book and documentary film, *DMT: The Spirit Molecule*. It was possible, I knew, to bring into my body a massive amount of the pure dimethyltryptamine (the hallucinogenic component of ayahuasca) by smoking it. I'd spoken to friends who'd done this and spoke well of the experience, which has the benefit of lasting only about 10 to 15 minutes. (Hence it's being referred to as the businessman's "lunch hour high.")

In July 2016 I was contacted by a neo-shaman with whom I'd booked an appointment months earlier. Nefertiti called to confirm that our appointment was still on, during which I'd experience DMT in smokable form.

Nefertiti extracts the compound from a special bark without using naphtha or other harsh chemicals. I intuited that her method obtains a slightly different and possibly superior product that — in addition to not generating a resin-like chemical smell when lit — maintains the integrity of the plant spirit.

Close friends of mine had endured disturbing experiences on DMT in which they interacted with elvish alien-like entities that appeared to suck away their energy in the spirit realm. I hoped that imbibing an entirely organic DMT would take me to a better place.

I arrived at Nefertiti's apartment and, after some small talk, she explained every step of the DMT ceremony that would unfold.

She served me a cup of tea infused with Syrian Rue about 30 minutes before the DMT main event, to enhance and extend the experience. Syrian Rue is a monoamine oxidase inhibitor (MAOI) that allows the bloodstream to more efficiently uptake DMT (just as does ayahuasca vine).

Nefertiti conducted a number of purification ceremonies such as smudging and the placement of crystals on each chakra point of my body. She then led me in a series of yogic breathing exercises. This might strike some as mockingly New Age and pointless, but believe me, as I prepared to smoke DMT I appreciated every single thing that offered comfort and support.

From a variety of options I chose to sit in a padded recliner with a back support and a cushion to gently support my head. I wore a padded black eye mask (designed by Alex Grey).

Nefertiti cautioned that the organic form of DMT normally requires more than the usual two or three deep pulls on the pipe, and that I should prepare to attempt four or five. She showed me how she'd help hold the pipe and light it, and said I should just focus on inhaling as much as possible and hold it in my lungs while she counted me down from 10 to zero.

She also told me that once I came down from the initial DMT experience, she'd play three songs on a CD player that was queued and ready. This music would guide me while I was still in the after-thrall of the Syrian Rue tea.

She lit the material at the far end of the pipe and I drew in as much smoke as I could manage.

I inhaled what Nefertiti later said was a very large amount of DMT vapor on the first attempt, which I kept inside and augmented with gulping in my throat, while she counted down.

"Ten, nine, eight, seven..." she said.

By the time she reached five my entire visual field was filled with sacred geometry; namely, a flat but limitless field of concentric circle designs, perfect in their symmetry, like the pattern of butterfly wings, in strong red and orange hues.

"Four, three, two, one..."

It took me considerable concentration to manage a similar heroic second intake of DMT vapor and endure another 10 to zero countdown, by the end of which I had fully crossed from our three-dimensional reality into the fifth dimension.

Any sense of up and down or left and right dissolved. Time and space disappeared completely. Another reality came on powerfully and I was overwhelmed as my body completely disappeared along with any sense of individual being.

Body: gone.

Emotions: gone.

Mind: gone.

Guy Crittenden: gone.

Somehow I still heard my guide's soft voice, which sounded like it was miles away, calling to me to make the effort to imbibe yet another (third) large draw on the pipe.

Guy... the voice said. *Come on! You need to take one more...*

I know you can do it...

Nefertiti told me afterwards that I managed to do it.

I don't remember anything of her counting me down. I vaguely remember thinking to myself there would be no fourth or fifth draw on the pipe (despite the earlier caution) because I was well on my journey. Some automated part of my reptile brain must have performed that final inhalation.

It's impossible to describe what transpired during the next stage of the experience.

I was in the place of eternity, and my human mind was completely gone. It felt like I was hundreds of years in that space.

I didn't really "go" anywhere, either. Instead, all illusion — everything that I ultimately am *not* — disappeared.

And what is left when all illusion vanishes?

Why of course, one's true and ultimate Self. I dwelled in the manifestation of my true divine nature, viewing and experiencing all from the place of ultimate Godhead, the Brahma, the Atman, from the inside looking out.

I was in the place of complete non-duality. Verbs like *went to* or *interacted with* don't suffice here. Unlike with ayahuasca, I was not *in the presence of* the Divine. With pure DMT I simply *was* the Divine. I was the supreme *it* (as, in fact, we all are). I was pure awareness — the *unseen see*r that experiences our thoughts, our emotions, our sensations.

Was this the state, I wondered afterwards, that yogis and deep meditators seek in their stillness practices? That the Sufis and the bushmen of the Kalahari entrain in their whirling or ecstatic dance rituals?

I would answer — most definitely — *Yes*. I graduated from belief into knowing, and from experience into being.

So, what happens when the small "s" self completely dissolves?

There is only One-ness. There is no "this and that." There is none of what the Buddhists call *the ten thousand things*.

Emptiness is form and form is emptiness...

But this was not exactly an empty place.

I was immersed in, and manifested, the most intense, jaw-dropping, mind-melting, heartbreaking love and abundance imaginable. Love sprayed into me, through me, and out of me, *like a fire hose*.

There was no *me*. There was only *love*. It was far beyond what an ordinary human mind can imagine. *At all*.

And it was also a strangely active place with much going on.

Since there was no *me* anymore to remember it, I can only remember fleeting imagery and feelings, mostly from going in and out of that state. There was no witness.

I recall being inside a giant clockwork, where everything is made up of luminous gold and silver, and everything is bejeweled and tinted with various wondrous colors. And yet it was not a mechanical clockwork, but instead a place where all forms were organic, and melting. And yet even this statement needs qualification, since every form, like a kind of visual music, was extraordinary in its perfection and precision.

Each emanation appeared with surfaces that seemed diamond-cut, or molded by lasers. Nothing was vague or soft-edged. Nothing was seen as if through smoke or a thin veil. Instead, everything was shining and bright and light-refracting and dazzling in its clarity.

As beautiful as it all was, it was also entirely overwhelming.

After what could have been an eternity the first hint of ordinary consciousness crept into my experiential field. This ushered in the first aspect of duality. I slowly began to gain consciousness of the experience as an observer.

Instantly I felt overwhelming gratitude and emotion and (my guide later told me) shifted to sit in a meditative pose with palms joined in front of my chest and fingers pointed upward, lotus position. I vaguely remember moving my body into this pose.

How to describe the experience of my consciousness condensing back to the place where there was an "I"?

My consciousness had expanded to the size of the entire universe. The return journey was like falling down inside the funnel of an enormous tornado.

Down down down I came...

...falling falling falling...

...condensing condensing condensing...

Thunderous whooshing sounds and torrents of watery energy surrounded me and, after a very long time, glimmerings of "I" consciousness appeared, followed eventually by the first nascent thoughts.

Down down down I came further...

The first sensations of a body began to emerge, along with memories of sensation, of incarnation.

Down down down I continued to fall, manifesting slowly again into corporeal being.

Eventually I found myself sitting in the chair, disoriented — this tiny frail creature, the size of a microbe compared to what I'd been, with spindly white appendages...

What are those? *Oh! Arms? Yes! Arms.*

Legs? *Legs!*

And a... *head? Yes, that thing is a head...*

Eventually I recognized I was back in my disguise, the whole universe pretending it's a tiny human being.

I sat sobbing, crying, aware of the absurdity of my condition.

Nefertiti later told me this whole experience corresponded with approximately the twelve-minute mark (*just 12 minutes!*) of Earth time, and yet I was far from done.

Around this moment my guide started the CD player and set in motion the first of three songs — very beautiful meditative recordings.

Oh my God! I remember thinking, *The music is just starting now and I have three whole songs to get through!"*

Just when I thought my experience was wrapping up, it was still underway, with lots in store. Instead of condensing back into 3D quickly, I languored in a sea of Syrian Rue.

This latter stage lasted about 10 or 15 minutes, but felt vastly longer. It honestly seemed like hours. Indeed, the contents of almost a whole five-hour ayahuasca ceremony were compressed into that quarter hour. It contained many teachings and interactions with what felt like the Creator.

The teachings mostly concerned compassion and my role in this incarnation as a protector of the environment, someone who can give voice to all the beings who have none in our human world.

Tears flowed and I cried deep sobs as I condensed further back into my ordinary human consciousness. Then, desperately — as the translucent realm of heaven began to disappear — I asked how to maintain a connection with the Divine.

When you manifest service, gratitude and compassion, you will be connected to Source, a telepathic voice conveyed, more through feeling than words.

I finally condensed fully and sat in my body in the ordinary sense. Nefertiti began to gently engage me in conversation. In time she removed the eye mask and I came fully back to the room.

Nefertiti and I then engaged in a long conversation about everything that happened, with me giving a tear-filled account and obviously greatly shaken. She recorded the conversation for future reference.

As I sat in the chair, gone forever was my last shred of doubt about the existence of a universal consciousness.

Nefertiti commented that I was wearing a T-shirt with Lord Batman Ganesha on it from the Thai clothing company Sure. That word, *Sure*, along with the word *Respect* on the front of the shirt, were emblematic of my experience.

I was now *sure* of my path, and will *respect* that it is real.

I had awoken in this lifetime.

I don't know how many previous incarnations I've lived through without doing so.

Gratitude gratitude gratitude.

* * *

It took me weeks to recover from the DMT experience. I was somewhat able to function in society and with my family and friends, but part of me was saturated in a luminosity, a divine drunkenness.

Be forewarned: being one with everything presents its own challenges afterwards.

I felt my values shifting again. Vastly.

Guy Crittenden was more than ever a sock puppet for a supernatural consciousness.

A line of poetry came into my mind over and over:

Strapped to a dying animal.

As the time-wave shock wore off, I found myself doubling down on my commitment to authentic felt experience. I wanted to dance the magic, wet grass between my toes and my eyes upon the stars.

I felt (and continue to feel) that no experience could surpass the DMT ceremony. While repeated experiences with DMT might teach me things, the thought of going back into that state of complete non-duality seemed... *unnecessary*.

Was I not here to take life's curriculum? To stare into the fire? To feel the blood — red light — pulsing through my veins?

Eventually I wondered if another substance might take me to the same state, but more subtly, more gently, and allow me to remember more of the experience...

In the autumn of 2016 I went on another paddling trip with my step-brother, and had the first of several experiences working with another plant that held wondrous, unexpected surprises for me.

Driving north past Parry Sound, we learned from the weather radio that strong headwinds would make it difficult for us to paddle out to our preferred destination. We called ahead to a local marina and arranged a water taxi to haul us and our gear out to the protected shore of a large island on Georgian Bay.

We spent the next six days paddling among the islands. The weather was excellent, and we camped in several places.

After several days settling into the rhythms of nature I opened the waterproof container in which I'd brought a collection of mind-altering substances, including *Amazonian Cubensis* mushrooms, *Psilocybin* in capsule form, and cannabis in smokable and edible formats.

My stepbrother eschewed partaking of any of this, so I decided to eat a cannabis-infused granola concoction known as a "space bar." We sat in front of a small fire in the late afternoon. Because I ate the space bar as dessert after a large meal, it took some time for its effects to come on.

As the sky darkened and the fire died down, over the course of about two hours I found myself falling into the medicine's thrall and eventually retired to my tent.

I lay atop my sleeping bag and Therm-O-Rest inflatable mattress, feeling a deep body stone that made it difficult to do anything other than shift my position a little. It was like moving in molasses.

In time my mind flooded with visual images, including the usual brightly colored sacred geometry. This reminded me of an ayahuasca journey, but the edges were softer.

I rode a psychedelic magic carpet for the next three hours or so. It was incredibly light-filled and beautiful, and I was thankful to have discovered that the neural pathways opened by ayahuasca, psilocybin and DMT were available via the softer cannabis portal.

The visions were similar to those of the other plants, but had more of a green vegetative characteristic (seemingly from the cannabis plant itself).

In time I met this cannabis spirit. She appeared subtly; more as a voice than a visual apparition. It felt like an enormous green goddess was standing behind me, and I had a sense of her rustling cannabis leaf costume.

She was very commanding, but spoke in a kind voice.

You have worked with my sister and brother, she said, which I took as a reference to the ayahuasca and huachuma medicines.

Now you're going to work with me, she said, adding, *I am the Master Plant.*

I was flattered by this invitation, but also intimidated. It was mysteriously clear to me that the cannabis spirit has the power to enslave her acolytes. I silently accepted her invitation, while making a note to myself to proceed with caution.

You cannot ever use me recreationally, the cannabis spirit said. Somehow, telepathically, I knew this meant I was not to smoke her leaves, intuiting instead that I was to consume her orally, as is depicted in paintings of yogis from hundreds or thousands of years ago holding cannabis leaf cuttings, surrounded by blue-skinned deities.

A light breeze whispered at the flaps of my nylon tent in the dark, its coolness balanced by a warmth that radiated up from the smooth rock surface beneath, which had been heated all day by the Sun.

After I accepted the invitation of this plant spirit, everything in my experience changed.

Whoosh! I was transported to a strange place.

I found myself inside an enormous egg-shaped space, the size of a vast soccer stadium. I marveled at this space, the outside envelope of which was made up of different bright colors arranged like stained glass in various geometric shapes. As with a kaleidoscope, the geometry changed constantly, with the light appearing as if from the outside, pouring through the semi-transparent glass forms.

Then, in an instant, the egg-shaped space shrank down to about the size of a small living room. As it did so, I felt an upwelling of love — that same divine love I'd experienced in the DMT realm. The fire hose poured again through my heart.

I struggled to make sense of where I was, and quickly felt I was in the inner sanctum of God's heart, the center of a sacred lotus.

I can't say how long I dwelled in that exotic state. There is no time there. The experience subtly and gradually dissipated as I drifted into a deep sleep.

* * *

After the paddling trip, I read Bradford and Hillary Keeney's book *The Way of the Bushman,* which describes in detail the cosmology and spiritual practice of the San people of the Kalahari. Brad Keeney — with whom I've taken a three-day workshop in New Jersey — is the only person of European descent the bushmen have accepted into their tribe as one of their own and trained in their secretive ecstatic dance and healing practices.

These revolve around a myriad of interconnected experiences, including the sensation of "climbing a rope" to God, and God's village in the sky, and also the healing of people by shamans whose bodies heat up with *N/om* energy. Tribe members dance around fires at night and reach ecstatic states in which they channel so much energy that merely touching a person can send them flying through the air three meters, landing unconscious. In these states, participants may enter into "First Creation" — the world before things are named. In this realm different animal and vegetative forms can merge and morph into one another. Ordinary reality breaks down in the original state of being, and different kinds of initiation can occur.

I was struck by the similarities of the bushman accounts of First Creation and the realms I'd encountered via plant medicines, with different animal, plant and insect shapes undergoing constant meta-morphosis. Interesting parallels also exist in the ways bushmen and

Amazonian curanderos use music and vibration to heal people, aligning their energies to a higher cosmic order and harmony.

But it was Keeney's account of the cosmic egg that gobsmacked me. At the center of the bushman shamanism there exists an *ostrich egg*. Seeing or experiencing this divine egg is the hallmark of a would-be healer's initiation. This egg, it appears, can be large or small, and the bushmen may experience it as something touched from the outside or experienced from the inside.

Was my cannabis experience of this same egg?

I committed to explore its meaning and power.

* * *

The next time I consumed cannabis I had much the same experience as on the kayaking trip. It was an identical journey, except this time I eventually journeyed to precisely the same place as ayahuasca — a place with a sinister aspect, the land of the dead. My breath grew shallow, my heart slowed down, and the visions were accompanied by a number of shamanic deaths in which I stopped breathing and repeatedly woke up.

Cannabis was now a necroptic, too.

Again the experience climaxed with my being inside the large egg-shaped space, with the changing kaleidoscopic stained-glass colors, the feeling of divine love permeating everything, and my sitting in prayer with tears streaming.

In March 2017 I went to a float spa in Toronto with my friend Bobbi. We were both inspired to create a cannabis ceremony in a floatation tank — me especially after having many sacred geometry visions the week prior, with no use of medicines of any kind, and also a visit from my spirit animal, which hadn't been around much.

I was certainly being called by Spirit.

About 30 minutes before heading to the spa, we each consumed three-eighths of a cannabis-infused jelly product. The total jelly block — which was shaped like a piece of Lego — held about 80 mg of THC, so we each therefore had about 40 mg of the psychoactive component.

The medicine came on hard when we arrived at the spa and I wondered if I'd even manage to change and make it through the process of signing waivers and listening to the instructions about how to use the tank.

It was all a bit hilarious. As I sat in the waiting area with Bobbi, the carpet became 3D and pulsed with different shapes, including snakes. I was getting higher and higher every minute!

After showering, I made my way into the tank, or "pod" as I prefer to call it. Bobbi and I each had separate tanks in separate rooms. As I was alone, I ditched my bathing suit and climbed into the womb-like container, as naked as when I was born. I'm certain that floating in the body-temperature water, loaded with salt to create weightlessness, reminds us of a longed-for fetal state. This might have been in psychonaut John Lilly's mind when he invented the technology.

It took me a while to fully settle into the water and relax. I should have worn the ear plugs, but it worked out okay. As I hadn't brought an adapter, my iPhone didn't plug into the external music system, so I just brought it into the pod and rested it on a safe ledge. I listened to Louis Gunny chant Navaho songs the whole time, which was perfect.

I also brought in a water bottle because cannabis makes my mouth extremely dry. I rested this on the ledge but never drank from it. Even though I got thirsty, I didn't want to interrupt my experience. I would have had to fuss with opening the container in the dark and worry about getting salt from my hands onto my face and eyes. (I decided in future to bring a water container with a long drinking tube.)

I quickly relaxed into a journey that ranked with my most powerful ayahuasca experiences. But it was gentler, without as many peaks and valleys.

The whole experience was one extended peak that ramped up and hit an awesome plateau where I stayed for the full hour in the tank. It lasted a couple of hours longer at about 80 per cent, at which point I was lying in bed in the dark.

One highlight included my sitting up from my body, half-in and half-out, in the spirit realm or hyperspace. I sat up without realizing at first what was happening. Then I looked down at my complete body lying flat in the water.

You can step fully out of your body if you like, the plant spirit said. I intuited that I could leave the floatation tank and fly around, but this was too intimidating to me in that moment, and I eventually lay back down.

This was my first experience with the energy body and its potential for astral travel, which I would later explore after encountering descriptions of the techniques in the writing and YouTube talks of former NASA physicist Tom Campbell.

At times my visions looked like an Alex Grey painting. There was sacred geometry, cosmic snakes, the appearance of a shape-shifting green dragon, and much more.

Sometimes the strength of the light in my visions was so strong I thought the session was over and that the internal light in the tank had come on, but it was the brilliant light of the visions themselves!

Many of the visions in the early part related to some journalistic research I'd conducted on the conflict in Syria, about which I wrote an article. This had necessitated my viewing hundreds of photographs of the dead bodies of young men and torture victims. I sought guidance about how to deal with this.

In my altered state, I was shown the deeper reality of the conflict — and all human struggle — from a cosmic perspective. I saw the Wheel of Life, the Cycle of Samsara — like a giant ferris wheel with souls getting on and off as it slowly turned. On one side the souls were filled with white light, alive or incarnated. On the other side the light in them was red: they were dead or non-corporeal.

From this vantage it was neither better nor worse to be incarnated — it was just a vast cycle.

The plant medicine intoned over and over this phrase:

Alive or dead
It makes no difference to her...

The whole experience was like a rebirth process. A reset. In the days afterwards I felt my personality changing. I became calmer and more centered than ever before.

Coincidentally, my friend Angela Elizabeth Marie posted this quote in her Kindred Spirits group on Facebook, which perfectly summarized the teaching:

> Each person is born with an unencumbered spot, free of expectation and regret, free of ambition and embarrassment, free of fear and worry; an umbilical spot of grace where we were each first touched by God. It is this spot of grace that issues peace. Psychologists call this spot the Psyche, Theologians call it the Soul, Jung calls it the Seat of the Unconscious, Hindu masters call it Atman, Buddhists call it Dharma, Rilke calls it Inwardness, Sufis call it Qalb, and Jesus calls it the Center of our Love.
>
> To know this spot of Inwardness is to know who we are, not by surface markers of identity, not by where we work or what we wear or how we like to be addressed, but by feeling our place in relation to the Infinite and by inhabiting it. This is a hard lifelong task, for the nature of becoming is a constant filming over of where we begin, while the nature of being is a constant erosion of what is not essential. Each of us lives in the midst of this ongoing tension, growing tarnished or covered over, only to be worn back to that incorruptible spot of grace at our core.
>
> — Mark Nepo

EPILOGUE

We should seek not so much to pray but to become prayer.

— St. Francis of Assisi

When death is regarded not (as with us) as an ultimate dissolution, but rather as a transitional (and crucial) stage of a journey, then the apparent Egyptian preoccupation with death becomes exactly the opposite of what it seems to be. It is, in fact, a preoccupation with life in the deepest possible sense.

— John Anthony West, *Serpent in the Sky*

It's difficult to know how to end a book like this.

I sit here, blessed with another day as a placental mammal with opposable thumbs that communicates through small mouth noises, on a planet spiraling through space around a small star that itself is hurtling through infinite space-time, engraving symbols on an electronic screen to share my thoughts with my small-mouth-noise brethren about how our consciousness may be altered by ingesting certain liquids extracted from vegetative life forms in order to gain knowledge of ourselves as finite manifestations of an infinite and eternal awareness.

The only thing strange about that statement is that it sounds strange.

My journey is still a work in progress. I've focused here on a period of slightly more than a single year during which I experienced profound personal transformation via the numinous through the modalities of Amazonian plant shamanism. The changes have elaborated since then, and continue to do so.

I don't know where it's going to lead. Will my relationship with the plants, and shamanism in general, taper off? I don't expect so, but I don't really know. It would be a shame if my serpent tattoo became nothing more than a souvenir from a strange year when I experimented with a magic potion.

But things look promising...

I'm exploring more subtle strategies — working in the scrimshaw of edible cannabis instead of the ceiling murals of ayahuasca. I'm interested in imbibing the most subtle plants that enhance dreams, like mugwort.

I've researched and plan to assemble a "dream machine," as was used by psychedelic innovators Brian Gysin and William S. Burroughs. (This is a cylinder punched with holes, that spins on an old 78 record turntable with a light inside, that you sit and gaze at in a dark room.)

It seems that even without such a device, with certain neural pathways opened up — or my Third Eye — I can journey sometimes on my brain's endogenous DMT. I aspire to eventually shift from three-dimensional physical reality to five-dimensional reality at will, without the use of plant intermediaries. I don't know if I have the talent for that, but a shaman friend of mine is able to switch to her "journeying eyes" as readily as you or I might put on a pair of sunglasses, so I know it's possible.

My experiments with floatation tanks are promising, too. I'm investigating slowly drawing down the amount of cannabis I consume before entering the tank, and am looking into things like binaural beats delivered via headphone while immersed, to shift my brainwaves from Alpha into Delta or even Theta modes.

My involvement with the Amazon Rainforest Conservancy and other philanthropies is invigorating, and I donate time and energy to make good on my promise to help protect our beloved Amazon rainforest. And I'm diving deeper into music, too. I participate in online discussions on ayahuasca and the teacher plants, shamanism and spirituality, and environmental protection, and am interviewed on podcasts on these subjects. Most importantly, each day I remind myself to be kind, compassionate, and free.

I've recently started researching what the ancients have to offer on the topic of altered states of consciousness, which could be the subject of a future book. This will no doubt lead to trips to India, in anticipation of which I've begun reading the Vedic literature, starting with the *Upanishads*. I'm astonished at having reached middle age — as an English major no less — without having read these texts. I'm aware of the supreme importance of Soma, a mysterious psychedelic, that permeates this literature. What evidence for it, I wonder, might be encrypted in the ancient temples I'll explore?

Was it a DMT elixir derived from the *Acacia* tree? Or was it (as I suspect) simply cannabis — my own orally ingested hallucinogen of choice these days? There's evidence for it being *Amanita muscaria* mushrooms. Additionally, in Persia an ayahuasca-like psychedelic known as *Haoma* was used, which combines Syrian Rue with extracts of DMT-rich Mimosa

Another priority in this regard (unsurprisingly) is Egypt — a civilization that endured for three thousand years, and whose iconography and cosmology maps extremely well on my entheogenic visions and learnings.

The *Acacia Nilotica* appears in Egyptian wall inscriptions as the Tree of Life. Were the Egyptians able to combine the DMT in this tree with an MAO inhibitor and access its psychoactive properties? As I write this, I'm on a second pass of *Magical Egypt* — a mind-blowing documentary series from Chance Gardner that showcases the work of iconoclast Egyptologist John Anthony West (who, among other things, re-dated the Sphinx). Part Two of the series is slowly being released and is incredible.

It's my speculation that a close examination of these and other cultures might help me offer the industrial world an even more energized argument for incorporating shamanism and the teacher plants into the core of its culture as we move away from consumerist capitalism toward something else. Perhaps, as we stagger on the brink of ecological collapse, we're poised to take an enormous leap forward into some greater mission for mankind — one that includes feeding and housing all the Earth's people, and then launching into other adventures.

Are we about to conquer inner space? Is some sort of transdimensional possibility awakening in us, hinted at by some of the less easily dismissed paranormal phenomena like certain crop circle formations or UFO sightings? Are the energy beings that appear in DMT visions somehow real? Are psychonauts breaking through to populated inter-dimensional realms just as the conquistadors discovered the New World?

Does this not deserve serious investigation?

Perhaps our technology is poised to seed the universe with new life — our life and that of other Earth creatures — transported on star ships we have yet to build, manned by robots and computers of unimaginable sophistication, that could colonize planets across the vast distances of interstellar space. Maybe the colonists will be entirely robotic, with sentient technology leaving us — the ape grandparent — far behind on our tiny blue planet.

And then there's the whole issue of death, and the teacher plants as necroptics. These have led me deeper and deeper into the realm of the psychopomp. With the near-death experiences, are the plants training me in death and possible rebirth? Do subtle choices await me on the other side of the grave, for which practice and mastery on this side makes available options of ascension denied to those who pass away unprepared?

The Egyptians certainly seemed to think so.

What am I to make of this and the other paranormal phenomena I've encountered, both with and without the plant medicines? The spirit animal, the remote viewing, and the strange white light that sometimes appears to me at night? Quantum Mechanics and experiments like the Delayed Choice Quantum Eraser suggest the universe is made up of information in a Zero Point Field and not physical material at all. If our world is probabilistic and made up of information and not particles, how much of a stretch is it to conceive of shamanic or spiritual dimensions as also made up of information — that they are as real as ours, since ours is also a simulation? Ayahuasca showed me repeatedly that we live in a Matrix just like the film, and now science appears to be validating that.

I'm indebted to my friend Brendan Ring — the Celtic harp player and author of *A Shamanic Kundalini Awakening* — for shedding insight on this. We corresponded about the ancient Egyptians and it was he who suggested Susan Brind Morrow's new translation and commentary on the Pyramid Texts, *The Dawning Moon of the Mind: Unlocking the Pyramid Texts,* which reveals that the Egyptians understood the body's energy systems in a manner that's eerily akin to that of the Indian chakras and kundalini.

They may have found a way to access the body's own DMT at elevated levels by cultivating it in the spine, just as yogis do with their postures. The *Pyramid Texts* are full of poetic references that include jumping crocodiles and lightning to describe some sort of sacred energy traveling up the spine, activating a liberation of the spirit that sounds a lot like enlightenment or awakening of the Third Eye (thought to reside in the pineal gland). The snake in the tree is actually the spine in the rib cage, and Egyptian aristocrats were buried with obsidian knives to release this snake when it emerged from their throats in the afterlife. Their mummification and entombment in dry desert graves was intended to preserve the body so their souls could remain immortal, but the brain was removed and disposed of before burial. It seems they needed a body to come back to, but not a brain that could entrap them.

Thought of this way, Egyptian burial chambers are akin to suspended animation chambers we might use to preserve astronauts during long interstellar space journeys. It seems dubious then that we assume no harm is caused in disrupting such tombs and removing the mummified corpses to museums. What if the Egyptians knew what they were doing? What if they were right?

Brendan Ring's correspondence, which I present here lightly edited, explains the yogic understanding on these matters:

> During the death process the pranas/winds that enliven the senses withdraw into the spiritual spine. Each one is associated with an element: earth, water, fire, air. As each element dissolves you will have an external sign and

a secret sign internally. So when water leaves you, you will feel thirsty and inside see a watery mirage. When earth leaves you, you'll feel light and see smoke. The other signs are fireflies and a flame like a butter lamp or candle, then white light, red light, black light and pure consciousness light.

After some time in this state the signs reverse and you are reborn into the intermediate state. This is the actual moment of death when consciousness leaves the body (not simply when heart or brain activity stops). After a time in the intermediate state they reverse again and you take another rebirth.

These signs are emanations of pure consciousness and, although they have no molecular structure, are shockingly real; they are called empty forms. Most people are in confusion with this when dying and so take uncontrolled rebirth.

Kundalini awakening and other techniques may induce this process while you are alive and so in this way yogis practice dying while alive, so that they have an element of control in their rebirth or may even stop it.

The signs started coming to me and they are astonishing. It took six months before I found exact corroboration in the Buddhist Tantras. They are in the Completion section of the Kalakackra Tantra and also in the Dharmas of Naropa and at least one Upanishad. My personal experience tells me that what is written in these texts is bang on up to the point of consciousness departing the body. After that, of course, I can't say.

— Brendan Ring

I'm indebted in my final comments in this book to Jason Hine, who has neatly summarized in several pieces of writing the state of the world in shamanic terms, which this book and my life aspire to communicate and manifest.

Hines writes about a period in the initiation of a shaman when the shaman may find his or herself exposed to the world of spirits and cosmological forces without any normal human boundaries. Their everyday egoic self has been worn down by the kinds of initiatory death and rebirth that I described throughout my twelve ayahuasca experiences and my experiments with huachuma, DMT and edible cannabis.

The shaman, Hines explains, is at this point exposed and vulnerable to a "cavalcade of spirits" and must try to make beneficent relationships with those beings that can help while protecting his or herself from those that could harm.

"This time in history," Hines writes, "resembles a potent and dangerous stage in the initiation of a shaman. In a sense the entire human collective psyche is a vast shaman, entering a death and rebirth ritual, in which ordinary reality is suspended and we are exposed without the usual boundaries to a vortex of cosmological forces."

Hines cautions that we might not survive this initiation to our "more robust connected earth based identity." Paraphrasing the poet T.S Eliot, at this time we may need to "proceed without hope because hope may be hope of the wrong thing."

We find ourselves suddenly living in dark times. What happened to the sense of freedom and light ushered in by the collapse of the Soviet Union and the end of the Cold War? The optimism of the Woodstock generation, and its ethos of loving one another? Industrial society is turning many places into charnel houses, and though these may seem far away, we're knee-deep in blood and hypocrisy.

Hines states, "We live in a period of 'divine madness' as the German philosopher Schelling puts it. This divine madness resembles in cosmological terms the quantum fluctuations before the beginning of the universe described by M-theory in physics, or the period of 'contraction' described in the Lurianic Kabbalah which occurs before the creation of the universe and before God speaks and creates both himself and the universe in an act of love. Nevertheless, throughout this whole process we can still trust in some deep, immanent, caring holding power of the earth and the universe, which exists behind it all.

"Now we are exposed to the chaosmos of irrational forces and wild spirits. The demons and their opposites, the anti-demons, the protectors of the earth. The radiant destroyers, between whose jaws lies the dark backwards abyss of time. The dead marching out of the moorland and into the city. Now we are exposed to the wrath of the unquiet dead." These "liminal beings," Hines writes, live in the relationship between nature and the collective unconscious. They arrive "in order that they can be known, integrated, recognized and honored."

Once they have been honored and recognized, they may transform into "beneficent and helpful spirits."

Looking back on the Year of Drinking Magic and my twelve aya-huasca ceremonies and their effects, it appears I've been drawn into precisely this struggle, which readers can take at face value or interpret metaphorically. Whether they're ancestral souls or actual soldiers, dark armies most certainly walk the Earth, and we are ruled by caricatures of all that's human, reflecting back to us our Shadow selves — inviting us to transfigure all, or with all perish.

I have seen (and have seen with) all the eyes of all the mothers that ever existed, whether human, insect, mammal, reptile, fish or bird. I've danced on the African grasslands with my indigenous ancestors, and felt myself a comical king, and have sat contented among my clan in the longhouse, chanting songs while watching the fish dry and the smoke meander through the thatch roof into the night sky.

I've languored in the clammy depths of mysterious swamps, swept by serpentine beings, and ascended to the candy-colored clouds of heaven, tasting my own tears as the golden-purple light of the Divine poured down on me like honey. I've pulled on and inspected stone monoliths from the Akashic library, and sat in shifting Aladdin caves of molten silver and jewel-encrusted gold, as some otherly conscious-ness minted thousands of beings in innumerable forms, and I've lain inside my mother's womb as she walked in silence. I've been venom-ized by spirit world spiders and died dozens of times, my breath faint and pulse indeterminate, and I've floated in the sought-for state of non-duality extolled by saints and sages.

How strange it is, but not surprising, that all of this is forbidden in our society, which wants us caffeinated and adrenalized for the workday, and distracted, numb or stupored the rest of the time.

What a revolution we have in front of us, brothers and sisters. Each one of us has an oar to pull and a drum to beat, a spear to aim and a soul to meet.

Thank you for your friendship, in this world and the next, and may your God or Goddess walk with you.

Gratitude, gratitude, gratitude...

BOOK PATRONS PAGE

Recognizing this book's sponsors from the
Publishizer crowdfunding campaign

DIAMOND LEVEL
Jacqueline Noble

PLATINUM LEVEL
Casey Worthington
Mark Sepic
Martin Millican
Timothy Martin
Yvonne Worthington

GOLD LEVEL
Barry Friesen
Carey Devost
David McRobert
David Niry
George Vojnovic
Jeffrey Johns
Michael Sanders
Raven Rowanchilde
Rick Vrecic

SILVER LEVEL
Aaron Harnett
Brigitte Habel
Carole Trepanier
Colleen Linseman
Daniel Cleland
Dave Fusek
Don Khalsa
Gail Cornwell
J.J. Rees
Jacques Tremblay
Jana Bell
Linnet Fawcett
Rose Oakley-Law
S. LIlova
Sheila Wilson
Todd Latham
Wil Eitel
William Metherel

BRONZE LEVEL

Alicya Scott
Alison Richards
Andrew Rowe
Andy Allen
Angela O'Hara
Anna Chala
Arnie Gess
Barbara McConnell
Barry Smart
Brenda Beattie

Carmen
    Layton-Bennett
Caroline Coyle
Carolyn Butts
Chelcee Aitchison
Christina Schlegel
Dan Fox
Daniel Smith
Davila LeBlanc
Dean Howcroft

Deborah Aaron
Denise Cormier
Denise Warren
Dennis Andersen
Dianne Boston
Dmitry Komendant
Don Hogarth
Ed Archer
Falon Webb
Gail Cornwell

Gary Sherrod

George (Bud) Ivey

Gergo Biro

Giovanni Bartolomeo

Guy Vincent

Harald Griesbacher

Ian Large

Jacques Chamberland

Jane Savile

Janet Norman

John Teubert

Karen Jeromson

Kathi Coyle

Kevin Meixner

Khris Crittenden

Kinan Debsie

Kirk Broten

Krzysztof Wolski

Lawrence Cotton

Lee Perruzza

Lester Alfonso

Lucy Hunnicutt

Marina Kanashevich

Marion Erskine

Mariya Prokopenko

Martin Millican

Mary Jean O'Donnell

Megan Stiver

Melanie Knights

Mon Lukas

Morning Glory

Nelia Tavares

Olia Eliasberg

Peter Veiga

Philip Vriend

Roy Moller

Sara Mason

Sara Lin Barron

Sarah Langdon

Sarah Dillingham

Scott Morrow

Sitaramaya Sita

Steve Duff

Steven Aikenhead

Sue Volpe

Suravi Anand

Thomas Howard

Tricia Sabo

HIGH FIVE LEVEL

Allison Breininger

Amy LaPrairie

Anas Attia

Ayrlie MacEachern

Barbara Andrews

Beverly Stone

Carl Stahlbrand

Chantal Scerri

Charles Jaffe

Damian Casanova

Debbie Ebanks
Schlums

Debbie Kasman

Desira Duong

Gill Pelage

Gion Marles

Guy Crittenden

Jane O' Hara

Justin Cheng

Kara Allen

Kilindi Lyi

Lana Sugarman

Lanee Brown

Linda Murray

Loloa Alkasawat

Lucya Almeida

Marco Handmann

Medea Chechik

Michele Ring

Negar Motamed

Nicholas Giagnoni

Nirja Chawla

Paulette Vinette

Paulina Leung

Penny McGlynn

Regina Scully

Ryan Kelly

Umair Nauman

Made in the USA
Las Vegas, NV
25 August 2021

28822491R00142